WHY ARE DUMB PEOPLE RICHER THAN YOU?

<u>Also by Laban T. M'mbololo, Esq.</u>

Influence: The Secret of Selling

As A Man Saveth *(Heal Your World)*

30 Days of Entrepreneurs' Series

Why are Dumb People RICHER than You?

Fresh Start-off: The Great Themes of Scripture

Influence: The Secret of Management

Laban T. M'mbololo, Esq.@Management for Results

Everything Revealed in the New Management World

Manage by Secrecy: The Hidden Key to True Leadership

Laban T. M'mbololo, Esq. @Selling for Results

Principles of the Top 1% High Performing Salespeople

Great Moments in Sales

The #1 Great Awakening & Future of Real Estate

Beyond The Great Illusion: 7 Sign's you're in a Toxic Relationship

How to Break the Bondage of Prayerlessness

Build a Great Future through Mastering your Mind

The Transparent Leader: First Client Meetings & Negotiation Tactics

The Key to Great Sales Success

The Deal was Great But…

FOCUS (**F**ollow **O**ne **C**ourse **U**ntil **S**uccessful)

WHY ARE DUMB PEOPLE RICHER THAN YOU?

How the Foolish, Dim, Dumb-Ass have Built Empires…

Laban T. M'mbololo, Esq.

Copyright © 2019 by Laban T. M'mbololo, Esq.

ISBN: Softcover   978-1-7960-5110-0
        eBook   978-1-7960-5109-4

All rights reserved. No part of this book may be reproduced or transmitted in any form or by any means, electronic or mechanical, including photocopying, recording, or by any information storage and retrieval system, without permission in writing from the copyright owner.

The views expressed in this work are solely those of the author and do not necessarily reflect the views of the publisher, and the publisher hereby disclaims any responsibility for them.

Any people depicted in stock imagery provided by Getty Images are models, and such images are being used for illustrative purposes only. Certain stock imagery © Getty Images.

Print information available on the last page.

Rev. date: 09/28/2019

To order additional copies of this book, contact:
Xlibris
1-888-795-4274
www.Xlibris.com
Orders@Xlibris.com
800850

Contents

Acknowledgements vii
Dedication ix
Introduction xi
Prologue xv

Chapter 1: How You Do Anything Is How You Do Everything 1
Chapter 2: Why the Rich Get Richer: 7 Things You Could Do to
 Get Rich Too 9
Chapter 3: Secret to Building Wealth: Buy Assets, Avoid Liabilities 25
Chapter 4: Stop Building Someone's Business and Start Building Yours 39
Chapter 5: Investing in Stock Could Make you a Millionaire 55
Chapter 6: Do Less and Make More OPM, OPT, OPW, OPI, OPE 70
Chapter 7: Plain-Old Dumb Luck 78
Chapter 8: What Dumb People are DOING that you're Not Doing:
 From Ordinary to Extra-Ordinary 83

Epilogue 91

ACKNOWLEDGEMENTS

The beginnings of this book stemmed from an inspiration to unravel what we see around us, and sometimes are not able to come to terms with the happenings. Much appreciation to the many people of intellect, entrepreneurs', men and women of honor who receive medals for works of valor and accomplishment that I have had to mingle with while on my travels in-bound and out-bound. Believe me each and every meeting I have had reignited the flame and passion of wanting to distil these ideas into a pearl of a tome; which I accumulate or come across, from the good reads I lay my hands on and the observations; facts and figures of daily occurrence's that can be passed on from generations to generations.

"*Why are Dumb People RICHER than You?*" seeks to unearth what the idiots have been knowing and doing that the bright guys have not been able to figure out and that this book gives insights on and how this evidently widening gap maybe reliant on some element of luck to transition your world; fancy putting in a few hours like they do and still be able to earn as much and get the best out of what life has to offer?

DEDICATION

Dedicated to the limitless power bestowed unto you, the power to love and share the infinite number of permutations that have birthed coruscating ideas which indeed have changed this universe, and the thought of a more magical experience to love more and often, to travel more to eclipse and discover the intricacies of the worldly cultures and to appreciate life more and draw deep from its experiences.

You mean so much to me; you are such a joy to my life, smart, fun & full of life. All this goes out to my daughter Sofi-Isabel M'mbololo.

INTRODUCTION

Have you ever felt that no matter how much you put your best foot forward there seems to be a dumber person that is making it and leading a more prosperous life? Does it make you wonder what you should do to improve your fortunes?

It's sometimes hard to take it in that in this modern business world there are people who are inches next-to-imbecility and yet they are making loads of money and enjoying a lavish, bountiful and more rewarding life. This can be heart-rending especially for entrepreneurial men and women and business owners to deal with. And the thoughts and perceptions that torture the mind are; why does someone who only puts in a few hours, is not as smart and is not as committed to what they undertake to do and yet they are still making more money?

Sometimes you even wonder if this has something to do with luck that you feel may have passed-you-by or there is a revelation you should seek which the dumb people seem to already know and you don't and how unfair this could seem!

Here is some consolation; You may not have control over whether you have good or bad genes or whether your streak of luck is running out, is fast-approaching, diminishing or that you may soon be the beneficiary of the next lucky lottery draw number, but one thing for sure that you have control over is the reins and power of your mind. Neurophysiology which is the branch of knowledge and science that deals with – the link between the mind and body – reveals that there's a compelling connection between breathing and the overall physical well-being that makes you stand upright, speak coherently and present to the world a self-assured you. A step further than this makes all the difference. Successful people today owe their success to an excellent-oriented state of mind and this can be the basis of positively revolutionizing your world. When you shift your thoughts, your life will change along with it and surprisingly the idiot figured this out and the brilliant men and women who are wallowing with dismal results haven't yet cracked this code! Food for thought…or is it time to shift our focus and begin believing in luck? Otherwise how else do you explain the prosperity of those that you don't like?

Actually for many years now there have been proponents who believe in the fact that luck is a greater determinant of prosperity than smartness or any deliberate effort directed towards search for wealth. It comes as no surprise that it's impressive how there are so many at the top who unfortunately are, so unimpressive. Time to figure out if luck could have played a central role in their elevation! As a matter of fact two Italian physicists and an economist have tried to unravel it. The 2 physicists –Alessandro Pluchino and Andrea Rapisarda – and the economist – A.E. Biondo researched and postulated that luck plays a dominant role over proficiency in your field of expertise in wealth distribution.

Economic data analytics reveal what you already know and which is no longer startling or disquieting; the wealthiest in the world that form the top tier 1 per cent have jurisdiction over more than 50 per cent of the world's wealth. The richest top 3 people control like three centi-billion worth of dollars which comprises of like more than what the world's poorest population of like over 7.7 billion people summed-together own.

Howbeit, what's the justification? More than often you will hear this phrase that the wealthy have earned it. Could this be meritorious or sheer avariciousness or a combination of both? How about considering straight drop outs from Harvard Business School and what follows is IBM the largest PC manufacturer in the world at the time approaches Microsoft for the supply of a newly developed BASIC operating system for their new computers, placing Microsoft on a clear path to an unforgettable and exponential business growth. Then going further on to push for exclusivity as the Microsoft software licensee for IBM's home PC's translated into all IBM products running on the Microsoft operating systems and an unending and assured continuous spree of racking in billions worth of dollars. Such was the case for Bill Gates. An intelligent and quick-witted product could have carried the day in one instance and an ingenious strategy could indicate triumph in another, nonetheless, at the back of the body, there are many hopefuls than the conventional perspective of enterprise would make us consider truthful. Is this a stroke of luck or could it be meritocracy?

The mostly prevalent meritocratic model of Minoan civilisation is hinged on the credence that prosperity is largely due, if not predominantly to attributes such as expertise, intellect, competence, briskness, endeavour, self-will, diligence and industriousness or taking a chance. Who can dispute this? And meritocracy or aristocracy – control by the deserving – seems so just, so fair-minded, unprejudiced, non-discriminatory, objective…

At times it seems plausible to want to believe luck to be the expedient factor of propulsion towards attainment of phenomenal prosperity, stupendous and inconceivable wealth. Nevertheless, it's not uncommon for people to downplay the role taken up by some external drive and compulsion from people's tales on achieving affluence, being well heeled and rolling in it.

We may be presumptuous or even surmise intellect, competence, briskness, endeavour follow the normal curve and the inference here is that there are many ingenious people as there are whacky people and in between them, lay the average people, and many more human attributes follow this pattern. However, material success defies this prescription and mirrors something called the law of leverage often referred to as the pareto principle and also known as the 80/20 rule, where the 80 represents the bulk of poor people and the 20 stands in for the minority composed of the billionaires. The richest 3 controlling like more than what the world's population of over 7.7 billion of the poorest people lumped together own. If the sharp-witted and shrewd as well as their diligence in work follow a normal distribution, material wealth however, is lopsided and asymmetrical or abnormally distributed. What's the missing link to this incongruity and divergence from the norm?

Other schools of thought opine that this could be as a result of confrontational entropy, chance and fortuity that, though a bit of talent is inevitable to achieve success, hardly all the quick-witted attain or even get close to the pinnacle of prosperity, and in fact are overtaken by the run-of-the-mill, common and mediocre person who certainly carries the day and the element of luck to the finishing line. Enjoy this interesting read as you envisage how it all unfolds, good luck…because you may need it and it does change fortunes, lets find out!

PROLOGUE

In writing this book I have sacrificed all other considerations to forthrightness and simplicity of style, for all to figure out and decode.

In this thought-provoking book I will rummage in and reveal why the rich are getting richer and why things are going to get even worse for the poor. The seemingly minor things are beginning to unpredictably cause large and sudden reaction and aggravating it to panic upon noticing the state of decay of things and the cumulative effect of series of small actions evidently delivering the ultimate thunderous straw that will break the camel's back.

On another less familiar aspect, the dumb are making more money than the smart ones considered shrewd, the grim reality and a hard fact to take in. But seemingly there is one thread of commonality that seems to play at the back of all this harrowing truth. Some external forces are at work that have either stolen wealth from the middle class and put it in the hands of the rich or things seemingly tend to work out for others more than they could imagine, once the proletariat, but today filthy rich and not even knowing what they were doing half the time. These external forces that will cause a lot of people to toil and still struggle financially or on the flipside - nobility, sudden wealth, positions of honor, a beautiful wife, a legion of friends, embracing the gaiety of children, a lavish life, showcasing a good sense of wine sipping a fine glass of Chatteau d'Yquem 1986, relishing the gifts of fortune– all hinged on the uncertain and capricious whims of chance and fate.

These and more agitating, decomposed, unsettling, unnerving, appalling divulgence revealed in *Why are Dumb People RICHER than You?*

CHAPTER 1

How You Do Anything Is How You Do Everything

> *"You can have everything you want if you can put your heart and soul into everything you do." – Zig Ziglar*

The first time I had the quote, was after I had downloaded the podcast app, navigated through it and had just began enjoying listening to podcasts as a perfect past-time while on the crazy morning traffic and especially on *optimal living daily (OLD)*, when Justin Malik narrated from a blog that struck a chord entitled: *How you do Anything is How you Do Everything*. I wondered what that really meant and was all about. After listening to it keenly and a few months down the line I came across literary works by Karlfried Graf Durkheim wherein he discussed his participation in a Zen archery competition in Japan. Durkheim made an observation that one of the judges assumed a pivotal role placing his focal-point on the face of the archer such that if he lost his collectedness and poise, it amounted to an automatic disqualification for the shot even if the bull's-eye had been struck right in the middle! Really?! That sounded so implausible and ludicrous. Isn't the main gist not to smite the target, does it matter how this got accomplished?

On a separate rejoinder there is a very high probability that whatsoever you are doing this very minute given an option you wouldn't be doing it at all. Even if you were on the most prestigious job and earning the highest within your industry of expertise and had to schedule some Skype interviews, get some appointments fixed for the next day's business meetings, return a favor from a colleague, you needed to grab a mug of coffee for an old friend who had just dropped by your office to check on you after many years, chances are, you would rather delegate some or all of these assignments to someone else than do it all by yourself.

Even so, you get home from work and there are some house chores that need to be sorted out, there's a meal to be made and probably some brief for some media interview due the following morning that all have to get done, it's easy to downplay their importance and find the easier way out to get the tasks completed. Nevertheless, and still they have to get done, no two way about it. Simply put; *How you do Anything is How you Do Everything.*

President Andrew Johnson who hailed from a modest and unostentatious background once while on his election campaign was disrupted by a heckler who challenged his proletariat and blue-collar achievements with the motive to discredit and cast doubt on his candidature. Without breaking sweat or loosing composure, President Johnson went on to respond regarding his tailoring and sewing profession, before his entry into politicking; "My garments never ripped or gave way," he retorted. And went on further to say, "That does not disconcert me in the least; for when I used to be a tailor I had the reputation of being a good one, and making close fits, always punctual with my customers, and always did good work."

Durkheim went on further to detail the final archer of the day in the competition. It so happened to be an old archer, so old that he could barely walk, and could by the hair's-breadth draw back the bow and when he eventually did; the arrow flew a short distance, forlorn and tear-jerkingly falling to the ground. Nonetheless, at that clear-cut and explicit moment, he let loose the arrow, Durkheim and the other onlookers were instantaneously forced to contend with a Herculean satori or spiritual arousal. The Zen master was nowhere close to hitting its actual target though it resuscitated an arousal and established a heightened consciousness, recognition, realization, appreciation...that strongly affected the onlookers. Is this really practical or could it be cultural and mythical folklore?

An account is given of a disengaged, conceited, opinionated and self-importance attaching adolescent. He vividly recalls arriving for school that particular day early but was quite irritable and on returning back to class from some time-out to find his teacher getting ready to put down some math equations on a conscientiously cleaned blackboard. He was all by himself in the classroom and probably the egocentric and self-centered youth pre-occupied about ladies he wanted to please. All of a sudden, the teacher Mrs. White opened the chalk box attentively took out a new piece and sauntered click-clack, up and down at the heels with every step to the blackboard and began to sketch. Her moves were calculated and quite intentional, quite impressive as she intimated with loads of endearment and caution that the lad was confounded and regained his alertness. He obligingly felt hanging, dangling and suspended and could have sat down there for as long as it took as he watched with admiration the creativity, skill and art on the blackboard as it played out. The truth of the matter was that the delivery was conveyed gesturally and unscholarly and something that's not easy to convey. Something was communicated that forevermore altered the perception of the lad that made the arrow and the target immaterial. Could this be the pointer to the clue to transform this world? Again a very real resounding; *How you do Anything is How you Do Everything.*

One more President. James Garfield. His conviction yielded to fruition and landed him a place at the Western Reserve Eclectic Institute. He performed janitorial duties and in reciprocation it settled his tuition bill. Never with a tinge of shame, he gave his all and was always jubilant. Within a span of a year he was lecturing a full academic load and still in pursuit of his studies. And becoming a dean at age twenty-six is no mean feat, this he accomplished. These are some of the impossibilities that become possibilities – at all costs and whatever is necessary – do something well and better than anyone else.

Johnson and Garfield transitioned from small beginnings to immense power through a simple act – doing what they were supposed to do – doing it the right way and with dignity and honor. They executed it properly because no one else wanted to be associated with the tasks.

> *"The road to success is littered by quitting but paved by failure."*
> *– Scott Sonnon*

At times the road leading you to the course of a breakthrough is treacherous and along the way you can easily get dispirited. We have to keep doing the things we don't like doing. Andrew Johnson had a polite way of putting it, there is no shame associated with a sweeping job, it was just another lesson presenting a splendid conceivability to shine.

Lack of Foresight

Sometimes we are so concerned about the future and don't find fulfillment in what we are given in the present circumstances. Many a times we abscond from work, take in the pleasure at the minute, go and revel and fantasize about sky-high levels of living. Habitually thinking this is just a temporary situation, a placement, means of earning a living, just a way-out, it's not me, I care less about it kind of attitude!

Matter-of-factly, whatever we do does count – no matter what, be it making apple crumble pies to feed the street children to building some funds for a rainy day or for any other pecuniary interests – even after accomplishment of what we are in pursuit of. Everything is an opportunity to perform optimally and reign supreme. Only narcissistic, self-regarding and unpleasant people think they are better than their current situation and the demands of the present moment.

Everything we are doing, wherever we are, regardless of where we are going, how we take and drink the coffee, how we fasten our shoe laces, how we handle a client, how we react to a bout of anger, how we respond to an infuriated spouse, we are indebted to ourselves, creative activity and to the far-reaching world to not only do it, but also do it well. That becomes our obligation and initial duty. When we take action, complacency becomes a thing of the past. We can react to life from a position of love, our fundamentals, instead of reaction directed towards control and manipulative schemes or responding to intelligence of an egotistical nature as a way of hitting the target at the Zen archery affiliated with accomplishment, joy and pleasure.

Striking the bulls-eye – the medal, the position, trade, occupying the oval office, influence, lacing up the shoe, stardom, prominence, drowning that cup of coffee – is not what life is all about. Each and every moment becomes an opportunity to enjoy life to its magnificent and magical fullness. When we learn to connect and recline in reality and allow the loving nature to embrace and encounter whatever challenges present themselves, we can respond unconstrained and innovatively from our innate feelings and not out of the fake, self-reflection and emotional reactions. We don't realize that is the moment life begins to unlock, extend, straighten out and greets us with relish, joy and gratification.

In an artist's life perspective they are given different forms of canvasses and commission structure depending on the nature of the assignment and the bottom-line is they prioritize each task. Whether it's the most captivating or the most highly lucrative, it's inconsequential. Each assignment is of equal measure and the worst thing is treating it with less importance.

Along the journey of life we encounter all manner of things. There are those that are highly-regarded while others are oppressive and back-breaking but never below us. Our response to whatever situation that presents itself should be;

a) *Diligence and industriousness* – indefatigable hard work
b) *Honour and integrity* – illustriousness, right-mindedness, trustworthiness
c) *Assisting others to the best of our abilities* – demonstrating loving care and making the person being helped feel they're the most valued person.

When life presents us with such choices we shouldn't be trying to figure out what has got to be done, because it's common knowledge; just make it our business.

It doesn't matter whether we get paid for it, people notice, whether the task is accomplished, it shouldn't matter anymore, all the tasks – should be treated with the above attributes – regardless of the impediment, the obstacles, the hurdles to go over.

Come to think of it, there shouldn't be any impediments circumventing us from discharging our responsibilities – whether tough or simple challenges, but certainly not too difficult. Whatever tasks we take up they require nothing but the best, whether insolvency stares us in the face, pink-slipped from work, dealing with an irate customer or making money and planning to advance from this step on. Given the circumstances, if we perform to our very best, we can take pride in the choices we made and stand nonchalant and assertive that we certainly did the right thing. We made it our business and took care of it – no matter what it was.

There are instances when people want to distance themselves from taking care of obligations. And you will hear words like, it's overbearing, it's an uphill task, toilsome, and feel you could opt to do something else! Call to duty bestows honor on the doer, elevates, its motivating.

He learnt from the best – tutored in the craft by his own father – even the back of the cabinets were of high-quality finish even though they rested against the wall. He took trouble and was concerned about the inside of his products and made sure they were magnificently designed though the end-users wouldn't peer into the inside. His name was Steve Jobs an American business magnate, investor, designer, then-CEO, chairman and co-founder of Apple Inc. In any design that was difficult and unsettled him, the late Jobs knew the clear instructions: *highly-regard the job and come up with unique and well-crafted items.*

We are all not endowed with capabilities of coming up with the next series of the Iphone or the succeeding style which is very sophisticated, coupled with exhilarating performance for the new model Mercedes-Benz, but we are creating something for someone – even if its repairing our own torn clothes. Every stitch especially the ones that no one gets to see, hidden beneath the undergarments, need to be dutifully done and should not be seen to be rushed or done in a shoddy way and shouldn't give way – we can take lessons from Jobs: pride in one's abilities and belief in one's self-worth.

Whatever situations we face life poses this question to us; "What's the meaning of life?" and that's according to Viktor Emil Frankl a psychiatrist and holocaust survivor. And our actions become the answer. Our non-complicated duty is to respond well.

Taking the right action entails being – kind, considerate, devoted, proficient and providing first-rate delivery, innovative – that sums up the question. And the ways to find what life means and change the course of obstacles into the right set of circumstances and a golden opportunity.

Habits of Dumb People that Smart People Don't Have

One of the predominant trait that New York based businesswoman Barbara Ann Corcoran, former real estate mogul turned TV personality as a "Shark" investor in ABC's Shark Tank, looks for in her new sales recruits is the ability to have 'thick-skin' and overcome rejection.

Corcoran says that she found out that the most outstanding salespeople demonstrated one common character trait which stood out and which is not hard work as the most industrious people were actually the worst salespeople, but high performing salespeople exhibit resilience and the ability to get back on their feet. Imagine overcoming the emotional toll of being rejected like nine out of ten times?

As Corcoran puts it – "it's almost like they are stupid" – they demonstrate an unending and absolute burning desire for what they have set out to achieve in their minds. They have an inner vision and intense drive that propels them to fulfill their purpose and dreams and nothing will stop them short of that.

Power of Persistence in Motion

As Robert Half coined it, "Persistence is what makes the impossible possible, the possible likely, and the likely definite." How does this apply in business and in the marketplace? Most businessmen and salespeople give up way too early. For one to actually stop pursuing a prospect they need to have followed them up between seven-nine times.

> "Nothing in this world can take the place of persistence. Talent will not..... Determination and persistence alone are omnipotent."- **John Calvidge Coolidge Jnr.**

Rather than being analytical of what's happening in your surroundings - "why does anyone need to live in a humongous home like that?";"he is a straight A CEO from Harvard University" – how about being stupid for a little while and make it work for your business and/or make that change in your personal circumstances?

Could you implore some form of being Dumb to change the fortunes in your business today or apply it in your personal life to begin enjoying some accomplishments?

Dumb People Understand the Power of Attraction

According to Lillian D. Bjorseth, to be successful the personal experience begins the very moment someone gets a glimpse of you…even before uttering a word. It's important that the encounter begins on the right path and therefore why you should portray a proper persona both in ways of behaving and outward look. First impressions can become a self-fulfilling prophecy and could influence your interactions as well as opportunities, since people decide ten things about you within ten seconds of meeting you. Business has never been casual, clients and prospects appreciate dealings with businessmen and salespeople who look successful.

Therefore it's important that your clothes be high-priced, smart, neat and orderly. The hair should look humbly done, hands clean and fingers manicured. When your outlook is good, chances are an even better feeling will emanate from the inside. It not only shows the world that you take pride in who you are, but it also makes you feel more confident. Feeling good and being confident has the effect of always keeping you at peak performance without having to worry about anything.

> *"You can't climb the ladder of success, dressed in the costume of failure." – **Zig Ziglar***

Could you act a bit dumb and apply it in your business to attract customers and give it the much needed visibility? - That photo shoot with that celebrity figure and post it on your Face book page or Instagram. It could boost your credibility and increase your visibility and bring you the clients you have been wanting for a very long time, adopting that tagline for every of your product that leaves your business premises. Would this be something that will make you more memorable with your customers? – We can act dumb and shameless and propel our business into the limelight and get that breakthrough we have been waiting for.

Certainly the accomplishment – target is important – but remember each encounter along the process also really matters.

How you do anything is how you will do everything, we can always make it our business to take the right action.

CHAPTER 2

Why the Rich Get Richer: 7 Things You Could Do to Get Rich Too

"All governments suffer a recurring problem: Power attracts pathological personalities."- **Frank Herbert**

Gross economic disparity is as heinous as racism, chauvinism and abhorrence of the disabled; and as pernicious in consequence; and quite reliant on a small fraction of backers who are of the belief that only a handful should have in addition, over and above what they already have because they deserve it.

Why the Super Rich get Richer

i) *Income Inequality Explained* –In 1915 Wilford I. King a statistician from the University of Wisconsin made public *The Wealth and Income of the People of the United States* which to date remains the most authoritative research first-of-a-kind. One of King's major motivations was to give an assurance that the wealth of the country was being shared equally. It was a rude awakening when he discovered this was actually further from the truth. In part, the findings of the study also revealed that the United States (U.S.) was surpassing Great Britain as it was known then, as the wealthiest nation in the world.

What unsettled King the most was that, 1 per cent of the population were in possession of 15 per cent of the nation's earnings. This was way back in the day-and-age of amassed wealth of the richest U.S. families – the Carnegies, the Rockefellers', and the Vanderbilt's –that paved way for establishment of the modern day taxation regime for fear that wealth inequalities in the U.S. would transfigure it into a European style ruling class.

Today, (August 2019) the rich possess a staggering 42 per cent of the wealth in the U.S. But what caused this to happen? The following factors provide all potential explanations – immigration, education, gender, the digital revolution, trade, demand for labour (decline in demand for labour in agriculture and increase in demand of skilled workers in building and motor industries), compensation policies in executive boardrooms and the stock exchange – proponents who say we shouldn't be perturbed about income disparities could be wrong.

Monetary and fiscal policies of unmatched scale were initiated to avert a complete financial meltdown of the global economy. The 2007-8 global collapse remains the second largest economic crisis after the Great depression. The U.S. was a beneficiary of 2 unequalled lengthy durations of economic boom during the late 1980's as well as the late 1990's yet 80 per cent of the increase in earnings between the period 1980-2005 was taken up by the top 1 per cent. Many economists were left baffled that despite the rise in productivity during this period the transfer of increase in earnings wasn't experienced by the lower and middle income bread winners. The global economy remains ripped in rags.

Meanwhile, the situation in London wasn't any better. The 1 per cent earners in England are taking more and more of the pay rises. Part of this 1 per cent comprised of married couples without children who require a minimum monthly earning of about $212,140 to keep afloat. And of the 1 per cent who have school going children, pay their fees upfront yet the rest can't afford and have to get into debt to foot their fees bill.

How come people don't pay attention to the increasing income inequality? One of the reasons is the tolerating belief in eventual social mobility. Economic disparity bothers you less if you are born in a country where regardless of your background you stand an equal chance of rising to the top and becoming president. In a research conducted between 1998-2001 of 27 nations, the majority agreed to the statement, "people are rewarded for intelligence and skill" in real as opposed to imagined social mobility. There are much better chances of rising from humble backgrounds in France, Spain, Germany, Spain, Sweden as well as Canada and Australia than it was likely to happen in the U.S.

From the authority of *Income Inequality in Africa* by African Development Bank Group (AfDB), other than being among the poorest parts in the world, Africa is second to Latin America in inequitable income distribution. The poor (who spend below US$2 a day) account for 60.8 per cent of Africa's population and possess 36.5 per cent of the income. The ones considered the rich (who spend more than US$20 per day) account for 4.8 per cent of the population and a hold of 18.8 per cent of the total income. The inequalities are reabsorbed by the middle-class (who spends US$4-10 a day) which accounts for 8.7 per cent of the population and possess 9.9 per cent of the total income. Evidently income distribution in Africa has traits of some form of equitable distribution amongst the middle-class and overwhelming disparities between the rich and the poor. Living standards have stagnated in Sub-Saharan Africa in the last 30 years whereas Latin America has witnessed its per capita growth decapitate by two-thirds in the same period.

Latin America is known for its adverse disproportioned wealth that makes it chronicled as a failed state (or a combination of failed states). Peasant farmers or agricultural labourers in clowns beg for food outside palatial homes and so forth. From the authority of the Central Intelligence Agency (CIA), income disparity in Nicaragua, Venezuela and Guyana is less equal than in the U.S. but almost at a level pegging with Ecuador, Uruguay and Argentina. As income disparities are beginning to fall in Latin America, the same is seen to rise in the U.S. From an economic standpoint the wealthiest nation on earth is beginning to resound like a banana republic, the main difference being the U.S. is so massive to check the geographical distance between the bourgeois and the proletariat.

China and India were some of the developing countries that have mushroomed so fast with increasing income inequality and only partially agreeing to a liberalized economy but blatantly refusing to go the complete free-market way.

ii) *London, home of the UHNWI* –The top 1 per cent are also the ultra-high net-worth individuals (UHNWI) and reside in London more than in any other city in the world. The people who fall under this category have a net worth of US$30 million in assets in addition to their homes. As per Knight Frank, a real estate agency company their number is 4,224 and expected to grow to 5,000 in 2024. One of the incentives for drawing the UHNWI to reside in London is the slack tax regime. From the authority of Pippa Malmgrem, once President Bush financial adviser said, "The crackdown on tax havens in Switzerland has removed these old options for new capital. As a result, there has been a huge influx of global capital into the UK." London's great history and tourist attraction, the recreation and amusement London nightlife accords is another reason.

Russian millionaires, at least 2,000 of them have found their way to the UK as the London elite who are also part of the UHNWI and whom it is impossible to even estimate their wealth because of how it is hidden. The Britons have left the Kleptocrats to patronise charitable foundations and make heavy donations to political parties which in essence means they are happy to maintain the current modest tax regimes on wealth as they are. They not only own properties in London but have also invested heavily in the London bourse and bought football clubs and where the rest of it is invested is unknown and remains a mystery. According to Russia's Federal State Statistics Service, by September 2018 a total of US$3.5 billion worth of financial assets were in the hands of Russian investors while the UK's National Statistics puts this figure much higher at US$34 billion as at the end of 2016.

In early 1993 wealthy Russians who because of their unfamiliarity could not be reported by *The Independent*, bought flats in Kensington at prices ranging between US$270,000-430,000. A month thereafter, a Russian tycoon relinquished US$1.474 million on a house in Hampstead and later bought all the house contents. "All he took into the house were four televisions and a van-load of carrier bags from Harrods." An estate agent reliably reported to the *Evening Standard*. An analysis by Knight Frank estimated that almost a tenth of the posh and extravagant purchases on the London market were by Russians, while Savills, a rival agent estimated that Russians love to purchase the largest homes in any group of buyers.

iii) *Why the Super Rich despise the Poor*–The justification for such disproportionate disparities between the super rich and the poor has got to do with how they view them as less laudable. Upon realization that the income gap has significantly widened, it becomes order of the day for the poor to be trodden down upon and treated as less deserving with deficient capabilities.

According to Princeton University unsuccessful people are not viewed as human beings. From a sample of the results of studies on MRI scans on brain reaction of the poor and on stimulation of certain parts of their brain, students mostly from prosperous backgrounds reacted as if they, "had stumbled on a pile of trash"

The people in power postulate that the threat to law abiding citizens is the poor and not the rich; that the poor have a criminal inclination, are moral deviants and perverted and therefore deserve poverty. If this was the case that the poor pose a threat to the wealthy, then the public should have concentrated its efforts on law and order for the poor. These tactics have been seen to take off the heat from white collar crime committed by the wealthy.

Those in power concentrate on individual wrongdoers effectively taking off the attention of the public on the issues of inequality and not demand an equal economic system helping the rich get richer and leaving the poor, poorer. To put the focal-point on individual guilt means questioning if they have satisfied their societal obligations – and not whether the society has fulfilled its obligations to the individuals.

Research from social psychologists in Berkeley and Amsterdam have revealed that when someone narrated their encounter with misfortunate or unfavourable circumstances such as infirmity or loss of a loved one, the wider the economic gap the less compassion was expressed towards them. Prevalence of such animosity towards the poor is evident in neighbourhoods inhabited by the top 1 per cent.

iv) *Extreme Inequality: When CEO's earn 541 times more than other workers–* It's not uncommon for news casters not to direct the question of the imminent gap between CEO's earnings and those of the lowest paid in their organizations, and if the national wage minimum had been kept in tandem with the FTSE 100, CEO's salaries would have been kept in check not to sky rocket to unimaginable levels. The unwritten explanation is that the lowest paid workers owe it to the leadership thanks to competence of the 1 per cent and they should therefore consider themselves lucky if anything for their current job offers.

But if this notion holds any truth, the richest would have created more job opportunities for the poor in both the USA and UK and this should have extended globally. By contrast, it's in Germany that unemployment has been well managed and hit very low levels for 20 years running yet the top 1 per cent in the U.S. continues to receive double bonus pay and emoluments than their German counterparts.

In regions where the 1 per cent is monitored, the people with the highest perks work for the common good of the public or compassion is manifested to the less fortunate in society at the least.

v) *Income inequality & Immigration*–Could income disparities be resolved by limiting immigration or by limiting massive breeding among the poor? Truth be said, wages and salaries in wealthy countries are dictated upon by immigration control more than anything else not even minimum wage legislation. Ever wondered how optimal immigration figures could be arrived at? Of course not by the 'free' labour market forces, if this were the case it would even end up replacing the native labour force with less costly and more often high-yielding and fruitful immigrants. Immigration is to a large extent determined by politics of the day. Think about it for just a moment!

There is no reason why the majority of workers in any wealthy country (take the case of bus drivers in Sweden) whose roles can't be assumed by Chinese, Indians or Ghanaians. A large percentage or all of them would be happy with just a proportion of the wages paid to the Swedish drivers and could execute with precision and deliver the same quality of work or even much higher.

Yet, it's not just about any cadre of workers like cleaners and sweepers, I'm referring to bankers, computer engineers, architects on the wait in Guangzhou, Quito or Nairobi who can do a better job given a chance and take down their counterparts in Stockholm. The fact is that the Swedish labour market is tightly controlled by their immigration laws and as a result the Swedish drivers and other ancillary workers can dictate the salaries up to more than 50 times than an Indian, African or Chinese worker could earn which again, are decisions which remain politically instigated.

vi) *Runaway greed can be tamed by a hefty tax bill or will it lead to a crisis?*–An introduction of wealth taxes could cut down on the wealth disparities just the way inheritance tax was introduced in the UK a century ago. To keep income inequality in check a top tax rate for the high income earners in an economy becomes necessary. For instance the top rate hasn't gone down for the past half a century in Germany and Switzerland which in essence means that the top 1 per cent earners take a lesser portion of their disposable income than they used to in the 1960's. In contrast, the US and UK top 1 per cent earners take home the most since the tax rates have considerably fallen over the years.

Top taxes do not increase the tax revenues generated, however they deter the greedy from taking bigger perks and allowances. For instance where a top tax rate is introduced off for instance 60-70 per cent between US$300,000-400,000 there is less incentive to earn more than this. By paying moderate salaries organizations can save massive amounts of money and the banks on Wall Street and all over the world could employ more staff to take care of the interest of the shareholders and at a lesser cost. Similarly *CNN (Cable News Network)* could produce more eye-catchy news and programmes with the big-names in media accepting less pay packages and still stimulate high productivity.

The flip side of this as suggested by other proponents is that governments provide welfare benefits to citizens based on taxing the super earners. This has the effect of lessening the rich's motivation towards innovativeness, creation of job opportunities and generation of wealth.

Facts and Figures

i) Half of the U.S. owns 2.5 per cent of the country's wealth. The top 1 per cent own a third of it. Source: *Institute of Policy Studies*
ii) Half of the U.S. owns only 0.5 per cent of America's stocks and bonds. The top 1 per cent owns more than 50 per cent of America's stocks and bonds. Source: *Institute of Policy Studies*
iii) 61 per cent of Americans live pay check to pay check. Source: *Careerbuilder.com poll via CNBC*
iv) 66 per cent of the growth in earnings between 2001-2007 went to the top 1 per cent. Source: *Harvard Magazine*
v) 36 per cent of Americans say they don't contribute anything to retirement. Source: *Careerbuilder.com poll via CNBC*
vi) 24 per cent of Americans have postponed their retirement as planned. Source: *Employment Benefit Research Institute via CNN*
vii) Over 1.4 million Americans filed for bankruptcy in 2009. Source: *mybudget360.com*
viii) 57 per cent of Americans have less than US$1,000 in savings, 39 per cent of who admittedly accepted they did not even have saving accounts in the first place. Source: *GoBankingRates 2007 survey*
ix) Africa is ranked the most inequitable region trailing Latin America. Six out of the 10 countries exhibiting gross income inequality worldwide

had origins in Sub-Saharan Africa, more precisely in Southern Africa. Source: *African Development Bank Group (AfDB)*

x) South Africa, Comoros, Namibia, Botswana, Angola, Lesotho and Swaziland feature in the list of the top most 10 unequal countries in the African continent. Source: *African Development Bank Group (AfDB)*

xi) The most prominent rise in inequality rests upon South Africa and the Central African Republic with increase of Gini coefficients from 58-57 and 44-56 between 2000-2006 and 2003-2008 respectively Source: *African Development Bank Group (AfDB)*

7 Things You Could Do to Get Rich Too

There's immense possibility to begin from scratch and still wind up a millionaire in any part of the world, though it's much easier in some parts than others. The fact that the rich are getting even richer is an assurance that everyone could get rich, you included just by shaping your thoughts and taking action and you will be on your way to becoming a first generation millionaire.

i) *When the Value of Life gets Cheaper*–This is a timeless secret applied by the rich. The richer you become the cheaper life begets. Have you ever registered how much is drawn from your private kitty towards catering for insurance needs? This item alone will produce massive savings. Once a savings of this nature has been established you just have to keep adding on to it so that the savings account can experience growth at an exponential rate.

The 57 per cent of Americans with under US$1,000 in savings and people falling under this broad category would struggle to keep up with insurance payments and could feel as though they are being exploited when it comes to insurance matters. The reasoning behind this is very simple. It's because they don't have the cash saved up to either fix or replace anything when it gets damaged. And your guess is as good as mine; they end up taking up insurance of all sorts to cover any and all eventualities.

Poverty Premium: Why it Costs so Much More to be Poor

- Medical insurance
- Motor insurance
- Home insurance

- Home appliances insurance
- Life insurance
- Burial cover insurance
- Warranty coverage of home items (laptop, TV, cooker, refrigerator)

What options would the rich take? They would have to cut expenditure of about 50 per cent of the above items simply because they have sufficient funds to carry out repairs should these items get vandalized or defaced.

For instance, if a dryer for some reason broke down, they would have enough savings stashed away that would otherwise have been taken up by monthly insurance instalments. If the car stalled and won't crank up anymore, they would walk to the local dealership and pick up a new-used car but in mint condition and pay for it upfront in cash.

If you had a net worth of about US$20 million and lost your life today would your spouse and dependants struggle - to pay off your mortgage, pay for your children's education or even fund a taxable account for your spouse's retirement? This renders futile the need of having US$1 million life insurance coverage. The rich wouldn't need these types of insurances which are ill-considered, unwise and misguided. Stop to think about it for a moment!

Amongst some of the reasons why the rich get richer and ahead of others in hiving away cash is because they cancel unnecessary insurance policies and save up these funds in good investment vehicles. Did you know that if you embarked on a savings mobilization plan, became abiding and consistent for the long-haul, perennially putting away $200 that would have been spent on insurance policies alone, channelling them directly from your monthly payroll at an interest rate of 15% over a 30 years stint will translate into a handsome amount of $1.4 million dollars?

Next Steps:

a) Cancel insurance policies for unimportant home appliances like TV etc. If it's mutilated even better, do away with it, many wealthy people seldom watch TV anyway.
b) Settle all pending loans and credit cards and set up a kitty for a rainy day. For instance if you have mobilized US$7,000 and the valuation report stipulated the value of your car to be US$4,000 would it be wise to take full coverage on it? It would be prudent

to increase deductibles to US$7,000 that will reduce the monthly instalments due. Apart from motor vehicle insurance, being self-insured is the way to go and will save you loads of money in the long-haul.

What does it mean to self-insure?

When people have enough assets that guarantee their dependants will be financially fine even upon the breadwinner's death, such people are considered to have self-insured themselves. This simply means having a self-funded plan that translates into having enough cash to be able to cover everything your dependants may require without the need of having life insurance coverage in place.

ii) *Ultra-Reach who Live Below Their Means: Warren Buffet & Mark Zuckerberg* –Warren Buffet's net worth from the authority of *Forbes Billionaire List 2018* released on the March 6, 2019 was estimated at $84 billion and yet he drives a used later-model of a 2014 Cadillac XTS an upgrade from his previous 2006 Cadillac DTS and continues to live in his five-bedroom stucco house that he bought in 1958 for $31,500 where he resides to present day. It wasn't until 2010, that Tim Cook CEO, Apple Inc. relocated from his small rental home into a 2,000 square-foot condo. In the same vein, 2011 is the year when self-made billionaire Mark Zuckerberg moved from his rental house into a 5,000 square-foot five bedroom house – both considered modest going by the standards of Silicon Valley and is often seen driving a black Acura TSX, valued at about $30,000. These billionaires are frugal to say the least and are onto something. According to Catherine Hawley of *NerdWallet*, "Many of the people you see with big houses and fancy cars are up to their eyeballs in debt." Talk about dextrous financial counselling, "live below your means" may be the parting shot from these business magnates that there can ever be.

The objective as always is to become rich, not to appear rich. A lot of people do not become wealthy because they are possessed with being identified with the emblem or signs of wealth and spend way too much money on this cause while they actually are of depreciable value. Their focus is bent more on appearing rich rather than getting rich.

The rich retain wealth because they adopt the spending habits of the poor. They make it a practice to drive in used cars, dress in moderately priced outfits and watches with only a few owning a second home, private jet or yacht. They know that you must not spend more than you earn, and therefore live below their means making it a priority to invest the surplus income in building a financial future – Wealth.

How They Avoid Debt. Millionaires avoid getting into debt at all costs. They have perfected the art of being frugal and will only make purchases that they can cover the cost of with cash. Cash is always preferable to them because it carries a zero per cent interest rate. They would book a holiday and pay for it using a credit card, and clear the whole outstanding bill, thereby avoiding the hefty interest charges. As a principle, millionaires will only incur and pay using credit cards if they are certain to clear the whole bill when the statement arrives and due for settlement.

Did you know that if you invested US$12,000 from age 25 to 65 your investment would be worth US$3.3 million? That's part of the power of living below your means.

Next Steps:

a) Adopt frugal living from the start. Avoid buying things on debt. If you can't buy it cash, then you don't need it.
b) Don't adjust your lifestyle with every pay increment or windfall gain that comes along.

iii) *Secret to Building Wealth: Buy Assets, Avoid Liabilities*–The rich get richer because they buy assets, the poor buy liabilities while the middle class buy liabilities thinking and believing them to be assets. **(We will burrow more into this in Chapter 3 and ferret out in more details)**

What is the difference between assets and liabilities? According to Robert Kiyosaki in his book "*Rich Dad Poor Dad,*" an asset is something that puts money in your pocket while a liability does the reverse.

It's not easy to put money earned through merit or as a result of effort and action into earning assets **when you can't figure out the difference between assets and liabilities**. On the flipside the rich get richer because they understand the power of investing in good assets and generating a passive income from it.

Here is a typical example. A family saves up US$20,000 and acquires a family residence through a mortgage. They generate a monthly earning of an equivalent amount of US$300 (US$3,600 per annum) through renting it out.

What the poor and middle class would do with these earnings;

- They would use this income to cover repayments for a new motoped or motorbike.
- This could also be directed towards settlement of next of kin's hospital bill or towards meeting their son's educational expenses.
- Blow it up on gambling hoping to double or even triple it or use it to a sumptuous dinner treat with family or worse still, go on a binge drinking spree with friends.

The rich get richer by getting every opportunity and money to work for them. For instance they would have taken the US$20,000 and got a passive income of US$3,600 and add this to income they generate from their day job plus other sources such as interest income and **buy another rental house and double the rental income to US$7,200 and they would keep replicating this activity again and again** thereby increasing their income earning capability exponentially every year.

Next Steps:

a) Put down a list of assets that generate income.
b) Embark on goal-setting for generating an income. Plan to succeed by purchasing assets and reinvesting the profits. Keep doing this over and over again and by replicating this activity, a passive income will come into existence.

iv) *Business Taxation and Financial Planning* – The more you generate, the more taxes you attract – right? Not at all. Though most countries adopt progressive tax rate structures so that high income earners face a higher tax rate, the ultra-wealthy take advantage of legal provisions within the law to minimize the taxable income, lower their effective tax rate and eventually tax liability without getting on the wrong side of either the law or the taxman. According to Ron Carson, founder and CEO of Carson Group and also co-author of *"Avalanche: The 9 Principles for Uncovering True Wealth"* he had this to say, "In general, America's wealthy are different when it comes to tax planning because of the options they may have with categorizing the assets they hold."

Here's a typical example:

Titus is a prosperous businessman and has US$15 million in realizable assets and has an income of US$400,000 per annum. His income is taxable every year at 37 per cent, the top income tax brackets. As a matter of fact, this is beginning to get into his nerves. To prevent being presented with such a mammoth tax bill year on end Titus decides to contribute US$18,000 towards a 401k plan or any suitable and tax eligible retirement plan. (Individuals of high net worth running prosperous businesses can also set aside tax-deferred money other than what is set aside for 401k or in retirement plans) Advantages are two-fold - savings for retirement and reducing the tax liability – another US$3,500 into a pre-tax health savings account (HSA), and a further US$22,000 to his special charity (or non-profit organization). This has the effect of moving him into a lower income tax bracket since his taxable income has fallen from US$400,000 to US$356,500 and this essentially attracts a taxable rate of 32 per cent which is lower thereby reducing his income tax liability.

To generate more income and attract a lower tax rate, Titus invests the realizable assets into dividend paying shares which earn him an additional income of US$200,000 annually at a preferred tax rate of just 15 per cent.

Similarly, from the authority of Michelle Fox of *CNBC*, Billionaire business mogul Warren Buffet, CEO of Berkshire Hathaway has incessantly singled out the tax inequality recommending rich Americans pay up more taxes. To support this claim, he has famously proclaimed that he pays less taxes on a percentage basis, lower than his secretary and other employees because a large chunk of his wealth is stacked away in stock as opposed to a salaried income.

Next Steps:

a) Look for your tax returns for the previous years and discover how much you paid, analyze and find out what happened.
b) According to Ron Carson, a member of the *CNBC* Advisor Council, "Explore the possibilities of categorizing your assets into three tax locations – taxable, tax-deferred, and tax free – to best protect what you've built."
c) It's important to understand the terminology "capital gains." Long-term capital gains tax rates for instance range from 0 per cent, 15 per cent, and 20 per cent. Federal tax brackets on wages range from 10 per cent to 37 per cent for the highest earner (for

2019). Short term capital gains are however, tied to the federal tax bracket.

d) Find out if you too could lower your taxes like the rich do. It would be a good idea to find a friend who is either a financial advisor or a CPA or invest in retaining these services.

v) *Direct Investment* – The ultra-wealthy don't chase for penny-pinching stocks with hope they would triple their investments or put their funds in an investment trust, mutual fund or index fund to earn a meagre 7-10 per cent and bow out. Instead, they settle for the long-haul, hands-on approach – investing with the objective of exerting significant influence and gaining control over managing the affairs of the company which could include a stake in the stocks (at least 10 per cent) or in some extreme cases for Foreign Direct Investment (FDI) they could establish facilities from the ground up, maintaining full control over operations. One of the reasons why the rich get richer is through direct investing.

Direct investing could take the form of the ultra-wealthy individuals meeting potential business owners who pitch their business proposals and ideas with a view of investing in the business. If they like the idea they would carefully review it and give the enterpriser the required funding in exchange for a stake in the business. For frequent TV viewers think in terms of the *Dragon's Den* a popularly featured *BBC* programme where budding entrepreneurs get three minutes to pitch their business ideas to five multi-millionaires where each gets a chance to interrogate the venture and offer funding and secure an interest in partial-ownership of the business, also make references to the *Shark Tank* TV series aired on *ABC*.

Ultra-wealthy investors have high-affinity for direct investing because they can keep a keen eye on the business anytime and can have enormous impact on the fortunes of the business by tapping deeply into their connections and wealth of experience.

Next Steps:

a) Clear all your existing debt and begin building up some cash.
b) Begin networking with intellectuals along the university forums and young professional clubs.
c) Start small and adjust upwards as you learn the ropes.

vi) Networking –About 90 per cent of your success or failure is hinged on the quality of relations you instigate within your personal as well as business circles. The more positive people you associate yourself with, the faster you will be able to get ahead and attract more success.

The people you spend time with have immense power over who you become and what you do and every reason this choice should be made consciously and with utmost care.

"You can't fly with the eagles if you continue to scratch with the turkeys" - **Zig Ziglar**

Before you Change the World, Begin with Yourself

Before making the big step to associate yourself with the right people, it's important to take stock and look at yourself inwardly to ascertain;

a) What do you eventually want to become in your life?
b) What people attributes do you want to mirror or follow?
c) What personality traits do you want to distance yourself and stay away from?

Big Decision: Scrutinize Your Associate's

Once you have determined where you want to be, you will need to surround yourself with people that will take you to the next level. Love yourself enough to do an honest assessment of the people who you spend most of your time with and ask these candid questions;

a) Among all my friends who are instrumental in propelling me towards attaining my desired goals and who is pulling me further away?
b) Who bolsters up the urge to realise my dreams and who scornfully laughs at my pursuits, teases and ridicules me at every effort?
c) Spending time with this person, does it allude to joyous moments or is it always a distress call?
d) Whose company would I feel better with and would provide inspiration?

Having established the above, make it a norm to connect with the type of individuals whose company triggers positive vibes and who you want to emulate that are pleasant, respectful and admirable. When out on networking or company events, do not just accept to take coffee with whoever is sat next to you, do not dine with the person standing in the hallway or alleyway, do not interact and converse with just about anyone. Be diligent and meticulous and clear-cut on the people you will be around as this has a direct impact on your thought patterns; will sway your decisions and how your association with them overall makes you feel, are very important facets of the quality of your life and therefore you will want to consider these cautiously.

The more connections of high net worth and positive people you establish, the better the chances of becoming rich. This is one reason why the rich are always outgoing, warm and pleasant.

Another reason why the winners of the lotteries squander their money is because they do not have networks and therefore do not have ideas where to invest the money and secondly, they don't hang around effective and enterprising people.

Next Steps:

a) Learn to always smile. This is a first step towards meeting people.
b) Become a member of clubs in your locality. A golf club or exclusive members club can be a start to where you can meet with decision makers, movers and shakers as well as opinion shapers of the city you dwell in.

vii) Lifelong Learning–Prosperous and well-heeled people do not rely on social media feeds on Tweeter, Face book or television for their information. According to author Tom C. Corley an avid researcher on the wealthy, almost about 88 per cent of millionaires spend not less than 30 minutes every day reading for general knowledge, track developments in their fields of endeavour where they have vested interests and also read biographies on successful individuals. Also about 85 per cent of self-made millionaires make it a habit to read about 2 non-fiction books monthly.

Next Steps:

a) Read a lot. Self-educate on business, personal finance, passive income, real estate and any other topic
b) that you consider worth knowing more about.
c) Always take notes. The optimal way to remember any new information is to jot it down, re-read and refer to the notes time and time again.

CHAPTER 3

Secret to Building Wealth: Buy Assets, Avoid Liabilities

> *"Wealth is a planned result that requires productive work and dedication. The Tanakh says, "The plans of the diligent lead only to abundance; but all who rush in arrive at want (CJB, Proverbs 21:5)."*– **H.W. Charles, Author of The Money Code: Become a Millionaire With the Ancient Jewish Code**

According to Wanda Thibodeaux of *TakingDictation.com*, if you want to create wealth, it makes sense to replicate what the super rich do. Getting rich requires shift of the mindset through behaviours that are propelled by thinking patterns and underlying beliefs. In the pages that precede, I will pin-point and make it crystal clear where to direct your attentiveness and mindfulness and highlight then extricate and bring to light the controversy in the way the poor, middle-class and the rich people inclination's to view money.

The wealthy buy assets, the poor buy liabilities, the middle-class buy liabilities believing them to be assets. Much of the distinction between the poor and the rich people is a sense of personal responsibility for one's own destiny and unwavering refusal and indisposition to take defeat in the face of failure or non-fulfilment.

What do you spend your money on? This should make your head spin and think in terms of the most recent purchases you made. Go a little bit further like a few months back and review things in a much wider perspective – flight tickets, holiday package, suit, new dress, motoped, train tickets, gift items, and new home theatre – think about all the things you have spent your money on in the past few days.

Make an honest judgement, **How many of these things you spent on will make you money in the future**? All of them, some of them, None?

In order to find out what class your purchases fall under, we will have to first take a look at what is the difference between an asset and a liability.

Assets vs. Liabilities

Assets are things you could own and which bring you future economic benefit.

Liabilities comprise of obligations to be taken care of that have to be paid for or are essential services that have to be rendered.

It all boils down to this – think once more about your most recent purchases, have you been spending more money on liabilities or assets? For the majority of people money spent on liabilities far outweighs the amount spent on assets. What stands out in the spending habits of wealthy people is that, a large portion of their money is directed towards the purchase of assets.

I like the simple definition presented by Robert Kiyosaki in his famous book *Rich Dad Poor Dad* that, "an asset is something that puts money in your pocket" whereas "a liability is something that takes away money out of your pocket."

The above simple assumption sets the pace on how and where to draw the line between assets and liabilities. Let's have a closer rummage and dredge up some typical items and check where they fall under;

Home:

Like most people there's a common tendency and strong belief that this could be your largest asset item that you are in possession of.

A large home acquired on a mortgage with monthly outgoings servicing the mortgage loan. With a simple definition and distinction between an asset and a liability, we will have a closer look at the home related expenses.

i) Getting a mortgage loan to purchase a home. Expenses paid out during this transaction – advocates fees, one time appraisal fees, survey fees, wire transfer fee, underwriting and origination fees, credit report fee, documentation fee, insurance fees etc.
ii) Payment of monthly service charge to the housing association for the maintenance and housekeeping of the common areas such as clean guttering, lawn mowing, treating the grass, cut back trees, hedges and ivy etc.
iii) Remittances to a sinking fund (fund created and set up purposely to repay a debt).
iv) Offsetting property taxes.
v) You dole out money for maintenance of the house and keeping it in good condition – cleanliness of the house, maintenance of fixtures and fittings, taps, check for roof leaks, check power sockets, replace bulbs, check outside lighting etc.
vi) General repairs and maintenance – a coat of paint every two or three years, check all windows are secure and leak free, inspect brickwork for any damages, check floor for loose boards, creaks etc, regrout tiles where necessary, run water and flush toilets in bathrooms not used often-times.

This list can go on and on. All the line items that have been mentioned involve an outward flow of money from your pocket. Going by the simplified definition of an Asset - something that puts money in your pocket and according to this home, it does not sit well with this definition of an asset. However, it does fit in the description of a liability - something that takes money out of your pocket.

The home becomes a sort of liability. To contend with this liability aspect the home that one settles for has to be of the right size and fits your needs in terms of pricing and space. Otherwise, when it's too large and begins to drain lots of money for this, that and the other, it fits in the description of a liability. However, the game changer would be if you have a property and are giving it out in exchange for monthly rentals, it then becomes your **Asset** and not a **Liability** anymore.

Let's have a take at the **Car** now;
From the authority of *Carfax.com*, it's believed that once a car drives off the lot, it losses up to 10 per cent of its value and an additional 10 per cent each year thereafter.

Because of the hidden costs, car ownership comes with a much bigger price tag than what you pay at the dealership. According to *AAA* the typical costs amount to about US$706 per month or US$8,649 per year to own a car.

So how much of the below items go into the cost of owning a car?

i) Fuel – most people tend to ignore this expense but *AAA* puts it at average of US$1,500 per year. To implement more efficient engine and lower fuel consumption requires; reduced loads, use of lighter weight vehicles.
ii) Regular maintenance and service – monitoring tire pressure, change of air, oil filter and lubricants.
iii) Depreciation of the motor vehicle owing to obsolescence or passage of time which according to *Carfax.com* is 10 per cent per year and the average new car will loose about 60 per cent of its value within the first 5 years.
iv) Wear and tear of moving parts – tyres, brakes pads etc. The older the car the more the likelihood of expensive repairs to keep it running.
v) Road tax, which also has other acronyms across the globe, is a tax payable by wheeled vehicles for utility of public roads.
vi) Motor insurance–According to *Insure.com* geographical location affects this cost item.
vii) Licence, registration and taxes – costs of government taxes, size and age of vehicle, local tax laws, fees payable on purchase of motor vehicle and annual fees.
viii) Finance costs – it's arrived at based on a five year car loan for the purchase of a motor vehicle.

From the inventory of expenses, it's evident that a car is also taking money out of your pocket and it's therefore not an asset and falls into the category of a liability. Going by the earlier figures of *AAA* the typical costs associated with running a car per month are US$706 which is about half the average payments for a house. The odds are, if you own two cars this will cost you over US$1,400 per month pretty close to your house payments depending on the neighbourhood you live in. The take home here is, unless you fall in the super rich class, always buy a car that fits your needs and not trying to keep up with the Joneses. A car is simply a mode of transportation to help you transition from point A to point B.

Ever wondered how the rich are getting richer while the poor have remained poor meanwhile the middle-class seems to be shrinking? There is a clear distinction between how the broke people, the middle class and the rich spend their money that keeps the rich getting richer, the poor getting poor and why the middle-class never stops getting stressed-out.

That's right, The Rich are getting Richer – Here's why…

Based on your understanding of what falls under classification of either an **Asset** or a **Liability**, you can make a self-evaluation of where the poor, middle-class and the wealthy put their money.

Poor: they mostly own liabilities and the expenditure are spread around feeding the liabilities they have created.

Middle class: they own some assets but keep acquiring liabilities and keep feeding the liabilities. They keep away from investments and throw around their money on to purchase and maintain things they don't need.

Wealthy: they possess an amazing ability to generate money from investments and keep reinvesting. They keep accumulating a considerable amount of wealth and assets that can be passed onto their seed, family, heirs and successors.

The Financially independent class: this class has amassed a great deal of good assets and the earnings generated from their investments are adequate to take care of their expenses.

And now a Panoramic View;

Normal "Assets" (Liabilities) of the Poor:

i) A car – it takes money out of your pocket as elaborated above herein.
ii) A "trailer' or "mobile home"– a trailer falls also in the same classification as a motor vehicle and depreciates in the same manner and lamentably therefore doesn't fit the description of a home.
iii) A boat or watercraft – categorized the same as either a car or trailer. A boat is commonly referred to as "hole in the water surrounded by wood into which you pour money."
iv) Lottery tickets – lotto, draw, sweepstake, gamble, risk – scholarly reports from a 2011 Study by *The Journal Gambling Studies* indicate that the lowest socio-economically one-fifth of Americans buy more than 50 per cent of all lotto tickets and the reason why it is advertised insistently in poor neighbourhoods. Benign entertainment, you could be swayed to think, however, the poor view it in a different perspective altogether. Lottery tickets are viewed as investments and the only way out of poverty and a ticket to improve their current living conditions and change their financial fortunes.

v) Furniture items – the normal type of furniture that is purchased by the poor has a short life span of about 2 years after which it requires replacement. It continually takes money out of the pocket.

vi) Consumables – these are expenditure items which draw money out of the pockets of poor people faster than it comes in. The items falling under this broad category consists of – food items, cigarettes, alcohol, drugs etc.

Middle Class Assets:

Liabilities Concealed as Assets - The majority of the middle class wealth held by the bottom 90 per cent of households are locked up in unproductive assets like family home and other assets like life insurance policies, pension/retirement funds and investment savings accounts which are available upon retirement or death.

It's very possible for the family to borrow against these assets however, the accrued interest from these loans milks and draws off from their wealth. Premature withdrawals from the pension or retirement account could set off early withdrawal penalties – forfeiture of interest or a charge levied on the pension or investment savings account.

Some of the Liabilities disguised as Assets;

i) **Bank Deposits of CD's** – could either be an asset or liability it depends on the tax bracket you fall under and the prevailing rate of inflation.
ii) **Bonds.**
iii) **Real Estate.**
iv) **Stocks.**

And now a deep dive to take a closer look;

i) **Bank Deposits of CD's:**

Deposits in the bank or certificate of deposits (CD's) are assumed to be an asset because it earns some form of return or interest. In essence when you take up $5,000 CD you give to the bank or financial institutions the US$5,000 and in return they give you a promise of an agreed rate of return for the period they will hold your funds.

Illustration: let's assume you take up 1 year CD of US$2,000 at a reasonable rate of 3 per cent, effective tax bracket of 15 per cent and an inflation rate of -3 per cent.

You deposited US$2,000 and received US$2,060 a year later.

The US$60 which is your interest or profit earned which is subject to tax at 15 per cent amounts to US$9. The net interest or profit becomes US$51.

But because of the prevailing rates of inflation the effective purchasing power of the US$2,000 diminishes and tapers off at 3 per cent reducing its worth to US$1,940. But one may argue that they received a net profit of US$51 right?

The effect of inflation is huge and can't be ignored. It can impact on the long-term earnings rate on current and savings accounts as well as the ability to fund your golden years of retirement.

But what is inflation?

It's the long-term rise in the prices of goods and services caused by the devaluation of a currency. But what causes inflation in an economy? There is no single, universally agreed-upon riposte to inflation, but its primary cause is the increase in money supply that outstrips the economic upswing.

In reality the US$51 net earnings or profit is subjected to the inflationary effects and yields US$49.47

After 1 year of loaning the bank US$2,000 the net effect is US$ (1940+49.47) which is a net loss of US$10.53

So what all along the middle class have been holding in their accounts as bank deposits or CD's concealed as assets, shock on them; turns out that they are actually holding liabilities.

ii) **Stocks:**

Upon purchasing stocks they **become an Asset if** (they put money in your pocket)

- The prices go up above and beyond to offset the inflationary spiral of the cost.
- They remain the same (in real inflationary adjusted terms) but pay a dividend.

When you purchase stocks they **become a Liability if** (they take money out of your pocket).

- The prices fall.
- They remain the same in nominal terms (but loose money in real inflationary adjusted terms).

Stock brokers take pride in making known to us that, "in the duration as specified ultimately the stocks have appreciated an average of 10-12 per cent per year." This sounds more like after factoring in the 3 per cent inflationary effects, the net effect of investing in the stock is to put money into your pocket.

Regrettably again it doesn't work in this fashion for the middle class. The middle class get the stocks at the top and retain the stocks until it gets to the very bottom. In actual sense they would have after the strong run withdrawn at the worst possible time thereby losing money.

To put more relevance into the activity of the middle class, at any given time there are market segments that are:

- Set to ascend (since they have been undervalued).
- Set to descend (because they are possibly overvalued).

Typical middle class purchase the overvalued stocks because at that particular moment they are the "hot" stocks and they end up selling the undervalued stock simply because they don't want to bear the loss any longer or because they are not entrenched in the "game" of stock investments.

Even despite the fact the "overall market" could have experienced gains of 10-12 per cent per year, the individual middle class investors are notably worse off, and after taking into consideration the taxes and inflationary effect they end up breaking-even or are hollow, inefficacious and unprofitable ventures.

iii) **Bonds:**

When you buy a bond it is an Asset:

- If it stays unchanging and steady and earns you an interest.

However, a bond could turn into a Liability:

- If it falls in price and surpasses the interest payable.

The same analysis on stocks is applicable to bonds however, the merits of holding a bond are that individuals cling to them much longer and the interest analysis is much simpler and can be arrived at easily. This therefore gives bonds more preference in terms of being an asset and has more potentialities to put money into your pocket.

iv) **Real Estate:**

When most middle-class people visualize real estate, they think in terms of their own residential home maybe because it's tangible and if they feel the need, it can be sold, so for this reason they consider it to be an asset and the fact that it doesn't depreciate like the trailer would.

Let's have a look at real estate in a more practical way. We know that it's not putting money into your pocket, at least not immediately and when it does; taxes, insurance and mortgage interest sometimes are applicable though we always hope to be smart and stay ahead of the game. Truth be said; for instance if you pay 6 per cent interest to the bank or financial institutions, and get a deductible on the taxes assuming the earlier 15 per cent tax brackets, in essence you save 15 per cent, so the effective rate of tax is brought down to 5.1 per cent. Generally speaking in the long-haul the house will appreciate and could be more or less that of the prevailing inflation rate.

Home ownership is considered to the best investment majorly because it does not leave you as worse off as the other options. In reality, because you have to reside somewhere therefore, it shelves the need of raising rent for residential purposes as mortgage payments is not something you want to skip on a regular basis, unless you want to loose your home!

The main disadvantages of owning a residential home are:

- It's not a voluntary savings plan.
- It's difficult to get into (20 per cent down payment or equivalent of savings is required).

The home may begin as a form of liability but in the final analysis it eventually transforms into an asset.

v) **Car, Boat, furniture etc:**

These items of purchase mirror those of the poor and are liabilities which take money from the pocket. The only difference is, the middle-class may be able to purchase better quality and therefore could last a bit longer and may not depreciate too fast.

What Rich People do Differently to Get Richer:

i) **Bank Deposits of CD's**:

The rich do not consider deposits in the bank and CD's as investments per se, but view them as places for holding liquid funds until such a time that they identify a real investment to purchase or remit payments towards certain expenses or obligations which need to be settled.

The rich always have their money working for them. Here's how; as known to all mankind, bank deposits made after the cut off time which varies from country to another, don't get credited until the next business day. A particular business mogul who had a deal going through at around 4:00PM on a Friday couldn't bear the brunt of having his money not earning interest over the weekend. He made arrangements with his personal banker to have the bank open and the funds credited to his account to earn the interest because he was expecting a large chunk of money - US$ 1 million.

The interest prorated over the 3 days period at 3 per cent would essentially have earned him US$245 and you would wonder how Dumb or what the fuss would have been all about? The wealthy have learnt their lessons early on to have their money working for them and would go to whatever lengths to secure their interests to this very end. It's amazing how people would run around helter-skelter to get things done for the wealthy client bringing in a large deposit past the operating hours. This is a clear distinction of habits between the rich, the poor and middle-class in how financial matters are dealt with and the very reason why the rich keep getting richer.

ii) **Stocks**:

The wealthy do not buy stocks based on emotions or telltale signs; recommendation or prompts. Their stock purchase patterns don't mirror what the masses do or buy because of thrilling sensations or for adventure. They buy at the trough of the cycle when no one else is interested. They make the purchase decision when the typical person would say it's Dumb for buying and when what they are buying is entirely unwanted (they will buy when its cheap since no one wants it at that point) this reduces their risk of loss and tremendously increases their potential of a gain.

The wealthy manage their risks by mercilessly and stony-heartedly cutting what would be considered minor losses before they become major losses. Purchasing at the bottom eliminates the possibility of the loss ever occurring.

iii) **Bonds:**

The rich and the wealthy buy bonds for a specific purpose after carefully having analyzed the risks involved. This could be as a result of consideration of the revenue streams it generates.

When a wealthy person wants to buy a Bentley Continental GT, does he walk to the dealership and just acquire one? Unquestionably and beyond doubt, NO! He would instead opt to buy a bond that would earn him a 5 percent return on the investment. He would then go to the bank and borrow at a low interest of for instance 3 per cent or get financing at 0 per cent at the Bentley Continental GT dealership and use the interest earned from the bond to make his car payments. Upon completion of the car payments he would still have his car and the initial principle (in the form of the bond). The decree and rule of thumb here is: *Not to Diminish or Use Up the Principle ONLY Spend the Interest.*

iv) **Real Estate:**

The wealthy don't visualize their own house as real estate, they think in terms of acquisition of properties – rental homes, storage units, hostels, apartment complexes, cottages for letting by the beach side–that will put money into their pocket. A large percentage of real estate comes with expenses such as mortgage payments, maintenance, insurance, property taxes and management fees.

Wealthy people know how to engage in real estate in the right way. They purchase properties knowing for a fact that the property will generate more income than it costs to own (positive cash flow) and they are not too worried what the market swings. When prices fall, they are safe, and even if they rose they still have more options. They do this by putting down the minimum required amount upfront and borrow the rest.

Appreciation

According to *Forbes*, the vast amount of wealth is made as a result of rising of home prices over the years. This is the "home run" where there is usually a massive windfall of money that people make.

In real estate ROI is a product of appreciation and leverage which offer enormous returns. If you purchased property for instance for US$100,000 and appreciation pushes it to the US$110,000 mark, then your property has just realized a 10 per cent gain. Chances are you didn't purchase the property in cash and used a bank facility. If you made a commitment of 10 per cent deposit (US$10,000) then in essence you doubled your investment and realized a 100 per cent return.

Depreciation

The title appears deceptive but, in essence describes your capability to write off value of the asset annually which drastically reduces the burden of tax on the money you put in the pocket, which also provides an assurance that real estate while still fattening your wealth, also offers safeguards. You can consult a CPA for the details of the tax benefit that the write offs offer annually from the property.

Leverage

Real estate naturally is simpler to leverage on the financing part of it more than any other type of loan as it comes with unbelievable terms. Interest rates are low (about 5 per cent in the developed world and up to 14 per cent in the developing world) with down payments of 20 per cent or thereabouts and loan repayments spread over 10-30 years depending on the amount and age of the borrower. Where on earth can you make investments with such great financing terms?

When executed properly, you could purchase real estate, enhance the value and then refinance to recover 100 per cent or more of your invested capital by simply constructing, improving, rent, refinance and repeat the cycle, CIRRR master plan. Even if in some instances you are not able to recover 100 per cent of the invested capital the ROI ranges between 50-90 per cent, not too bad either.

Real estate gets even better because you actually get finance from the bank or financial institutions; repay the finance with the rent collected from tenants and keep the difference, where else can you get this from an investment?

Forced equity

This offers an incredible way to create wealth commonly done through purchasing a property, and upgrading its condition usually paying below market price then making additions such as appliances like air conditioning, flooring, renovations of gypsum ceiling, additional LED lighting and paint works. Majority of investors have the tendency to force equity through addition of features that lack in an ideal property to make it more vibrant e.g. addition of bath cubicles, extra bedrooms, improving the lighting etc.

Inflation

The secret to creating phenomenal wealth in real estate, lies in the fact that the main large expense items remain static (mortgage, property taxes, maintenance fees) for the longest time you may own the property, while the rents and the value of the homes keeps rising (owing to inflation) then you begin to see the big picture.

This is an eye-opener as to why there are gains to be made in real estate which many people don't comprehend very well which could create you enormous wealth.

v) **Mortgages:**

Are mortgages considered as assets or liabilities? Seems like a Dumb question! For most middle-class the thought of mortgage refers to ownership of own- houses. There is this common belief that house ownership is possession of an asset, just depends on how you view it.

The super rich use mortgage loans with ridiculously low interest rates to their advantage. So why get a mortgage when you can afford to buy an expensive house in cash? Instead of tying up their money in purchasing a home the rich use this money for more profitable ventures. According to Greg McBride, a senior analyst at *Bankrate.com*, "When you are able to borrow at an interest rate that's below the rate of inflation you're essentially borrowing for free."

But how do the super rich get such low rates? These kinds of loans bear low interest rates and remain only accessible to buyers who are low risk to the banks and financial institutions – the super rich, corporate executives. (It's highly unlikely that a billionaire would default on a payment). Most of these types of mortgages are adjustable, meaning the rates could go up. Should the interest shoot up or if it becomes too high to service the mortgage, the super rich can bounce and buy their homes outright.

Such mortgages are not a mainstream product and are offered at preferential rates only to the wealthy which is another reason why the rich are getting richer. *Bloomberg* once reported that Mark Zuckerberg the CEO of *Face book* had refinanced the mortgage for his house, The Palo Alto with a

30 year adjustable mortgage loan at a stunning rate of 1.05 per cent, less than half the average.

Ultimate Thoughts:

By expanding your network and circle of influence with people with a more powerful sense of finance, the more their mindset will begin to rub off on you. People who enjoy riches are also able to look at life in the long-haul rather than getting carried away in the heat of the moment, express willingness to learn and accept help along their financial journey.

CHAPTER 4

Stop Building Someone's Business and Start Building Yours

"I knew that if I failed I wouldn't regret that, but I knew the one thing I might regret is not trying." – **Jeff Bezos, *Amazon Founder & CEO***

You will never regret why you stumbled into this book and flipped the pages to even get to this chapter. Are you busy building somebody else's dream, or are your efforts directed towards building your own? Your life will never be the same when you awaken to this reality. Once you uncover the findings of this chapter, you will then understand why. Why are there individuals who seem to attract immeasurable riches into their lives while others who are as capable or competent, suffer from extreme poverty or the lack of prosperity in absolute terms and relish in engaging in 9-5 day jobs to just collect a pay check? You will make an interesting discovery through this chapter, that it has nothing to do with competence, repute, environment, intelligence, geography or physical prowess. In the pages that ensue, I will unveil why if you are working for someone else, you are only helping them with their dream, but if you want to be rich, you are on an assured path of hurting yourself, what about you and what you want to do?

When your alarm sets off and sounds in the morning, is it met with excitement to roll out of bed and get started or do you drag your feet, dread the beginning of another day doing mundane things that you don't enjoy doing and just do them to earn that end month pay check? Well, it pretty much gives you the pay check that you require to get on with life, but never the pleasure, accomplishment, challenge it brings along with it or that extra income you truly need to make a difference in your life.

A frequent pay check is spine-chilling and blood-curdling to give up. I have been there myself and can personally attest to this safety-zone you get confined into by perennially receiving a pay check, yet the worth involved in creation of a business and life that you love, will truly propel you to look up to waking up each day in pursuit of your own dreams.

Why is Getting a Job so Dumb?

1) *Get Paid whether you Work or Not*–Being employed is so idiotic because essentially you restrict yourself towards being paid only when you are working. The problem is, the majority of people have been brainwashed into thinking it's intelligent and so cool to get paid when working. How about considering the alternative of getting better paid even while not working? Won't you fancy earning while playing with the children, dining out with friends, scuba diving, while asleep or even when on a holiday abroad and still get paid 24/7? If your plants grow overnight when you are not even watching over them, why not replicate that with your bank account? Calculative and shrewd people establish systems that create passive income 24/7. Some of the options include website construction, becoming an investor, beginning an enterprise or even generating royalty income from innovative and creative works. In this manner the system delivers the value to the intended clients or targeted customer base and once rolled out, it generates a stream of income whether you attend to it or not. This way, the higher percentage of your time can be dedicated towards increasing the income generated. Formation of a website is a good example, registration of the domain name is less than US$10 and anything after that are straight profits. At the same time, this frees up time to make additional income from other multiple sources of income (MSI's).

2) *The Rich pay Less Tax Applying Powers of a Corporation*– Income earned by an employee is the most heavily taxed anywhere in the world. According to Robert Kiyosaki in his book *Rich Dad Poor Dad*, the

reality is such that the rich are not taxed and the educated upper income middle-class are the ones who pay for the poor. The wealthy outsmarted the intellectuals and eventually levied taxes on the middle-class for the single reason that they were well versed with the power of money which isn't common knowledge disseminated in schools. The rich have corporations which isn't a real person but just a file with a mound of legal documents that sits up in an attorney's office and registered with a state government agency offices, that makes it a "legal person" that can sue, get sued and even own properties. This is how the wealthy protect their riches because the tax rates for a corporation are also much lower than income tax rates applicable to individuals.

If employees took trouble to understand how the wealthy have a master plan and play it in a certain way they would be on their way to attaining financial independence. The problem is that the learned middle-class are so unenlightened and are the very ones who rise up early to go and work so diligently and pay their taxes religiously in fact, it is recovered at source even before they lay their hands on the proceeds of their pay check.

Businessmen possess the knowledge of the law and how the system works and in essence know how to get their money to work for them. And this explains why they would go to extents of retaining the services of smart tax advocates and CPA's, because it works out cheaper to pay these professionals than pay a whole load of taxes to the government.

3) *Way too Risky* – it's the belief of most employees that happens to be a direct result of conditioning that, seeking employment is more secure and the safest way to support themselves and their families. It could even make you view the thought of starting a business as a disastrous prognosis.

However, the notion of deriving income from a job is unwise and misguided. Can you have security when you don't have control and the fact that you could easily get sent home by the resounding of these 3 words, "you are fired"?

Does having more than 10 MSI's guarantee you more security than a single income stream from a job? Having a job could be equated to gambling because the loss of a job could send everything downward spiralling if you get pink-slipped.

4) *Limitations with Experience* – the main problem with getting experience on the job is that initially you learn a lot at the beginning, but as time

goes by you start regurgitating the same experience over and over again and that's when you begin to stagnate.

Retaining such a job is costly because you miss out on much more valuable experience and with time the limited skills and experience become obsolete. Ask yourself this question; will your job be in existence 10-20 years down the line, what about the experience you are gaining now, will it still be relevant?

Its worth considering this, which experience is worth pursuing? Would it be knowledge do perform well at a certain job which is - trading your time for paid income - or would it be knowledge and expertise gained on how to enjoy life-long financial independence without ever having the thoughts of finding a job or dealing with an employer indefinitely and the possible wrath of a job-loss?

5) *Restricted Socializations* – For the majority of those in employment this becomes their main point of networking. They spend a good portion of their time in the camaraderie of colleagues and friends at work. This kind of lewd and interbred relationship becomes a networking deadlock.

Just imagine a day out meeting a different clique of people and possible strangers deliberating on the next possible inventions of *Microsoft*, the user-friendliness of the newly online payment gateway systems for *Amazon.com!*

It can be life-changing to get out there and network with the people you choose to and not those your employer decides on your behalf. Make this decision carefully and once you have determined where you want to be, you will need to surround yourself with people that will move you to the next level. Love yourself enough to do an honest assessment of the people who you spend most of your time with. Look for them at networking meetings, corporate events and launches, press events and conferences.

I attended one of Tony Robbins' motivational workshops in Teecom, Media City, Dubai, UAE on March 4, 2016 and he had this to say, "Whoever you spend time with, you become who they are." You should also leverage on your already established networks, seminars and workshops, trade fairs and exhibitions, participation in walks, charitable and community events to regularly oil and add onto your networks. The unique fact still remains that real success hinges on establishing and maintaining great relationships.

6) *Losing your Freedom* – It takes deliberate continuous effort to break human freewill and attain conversion into a tamed employee through a series of inductions and endless non-sensical rules and regulations

by handing new employees voluminous policy manuals to be adhered to with their signed autograph as attestations to ensure compliance when joining in and into the foreseeable future.

This instils fear upon the new employees and enforces discipline and gets one step closer to confirming that obeying the master's sovereignty without querying will not attract reprimands. With a stir of a bit of office politics and supplicated to like-minded colleagues the employer would have a reason to celebrate a new addition and slave-of-the-mind convert.

And because it's dangerous to have an employee operating on own-independent thoughts, induction on obedience including a dress code to adhere to, acceptable mannerisms in speech and movement would be administered.

The only way to do away with such silly rules and regulations is by building your own business where you can be rest assured of your freedom and human freewill and where your smartness operates without limitations, you do what you love and have as much fun and take holidays as you please and still rack in the millions.

7) *Instil Cowardice* – It will come as no surprise to you that employees display tendencies to whine endlessly about company issues and work-related challenges. Matter-of-factly, they are not venting out because they are looking for solutions, but just the mere fact of wanting to apportion blame on others on what went wrong, confirming that employment drains the free will out and turns employees into spineless cowards who will not even dare to tell off their bosses, even when they were inadvertently doing something detrimental to the company.

The truth is that chances of being the 10th con when you spend all your valuable time with 9 cons are very probable. When you work with cowards all day, it will begin to rub off on you. Hang out with people you learn from, people who build you, empower you and make you a better person. Be sure you hang with the people who are going places. Establish real relationships and work together. Take time to know and research the people you hang out with. Don't just trust everyone on the first meeting. Just as you need to establish trust with your community, expect the same of those you bring into your inner circle. Remember trust is expensive and you therefore don't expect to find it in cheap people.

Your greatest fear becomes finding out who you have become. First to go out of the window is honesty…then courage…followed by integrity and honour…and in the end you loose your independent free will. In short, you traded your humanity in exchange for an illusion of a job and you have turn out into who you are and look so emaciated. Remember, it's never too late to regain your composure and courage once again.

How to Start and Build your Own Business

Doing the thing that you enjoy the most entails gaining the requisite knowledge, advice and real life experiences that will set you free from the chains of a day job and that are revealed in the below *Secrets for Relinquishing the Pay check-to-Pay check Life* to create a more flourishing and prosperous business:

i) An *easy-to-follow* guide for setting up your business while still working on your day job.
ii) How to identify and leverage on your unique gifts and talents to begin your business and attract the right clients for your business.
iii) Obstacles and how to overcome them on your journey to prosperity.
iv) A wealth of success tips and guidelines that will gravitate you towards accomplishing your desired goals.

Secrets for Relinquishing the Pay check-to-Pay check Life

Let's now dredge up more:

i) **An easy-to-follow guide for setting up your business while still working on your day job.**

From the authority of research from *Bentley University*, more than 66 per cent of Millennials expressed desire to start their own businesses. As of 2013, only 3.6 per cent of businesses were owned by individuals less than 30 years of age suggesting there is a large discrepancy between those who have the desire to establish the businesses and those that are actually able to get them to get off the ground.

There has never before been such a surge of high numbers of young enterprising individuals wanting to enter into the business world to become own-bosses. Their business models range from; start-up business founders, authors, web and app developers, freelance content marketers, business consultants, strategy consultants, financial advisory consultants, ICT consultants, management consultants etc.

The most interesting part of this journey is that, these entrepreneurs have been able to transform small scale businesses into the million range, is this evidently sufficient proof for you to still want to start building your own business as you plan to quit your paid day job?

The main advantage is having an income that could fund the new enterprising idea while concentrating on deliverables with the highest impact and easing off pressure on yourself, which bears the potentiality of launching and pulling off a successful business venture while still working.

Here's how to execute the plan while still keeping up with your day job:

1) *Getting the Commitment*–Begin with yourself and question how desperately do you want to be in business because this can take a toll on your relationship as many a times you will be required to take tough decisions.

    Take stock of the activities and commitments that revolve around your life and the amount of time spent on each during a week period. Mark the ones that you can begin to considerably reduce your time on and notify the people who would be supportive, that you are taking time off to concentrate on a new project that's close to your heart. First things first, the easy things to cut back on would include;

    a) Time spent on social media especially Face book, LinkedIn, Instagram and Twitter handles.
    b) Time spent watching TV.
    c) Time spent socializing with friends and playing games.

In order for you to be able to see tangible results, you will need to free up more time sooner than later.

2) *Take inventory of your skill-set, Capabilities and Shortcomings* –In this stage list all the skill-set, knowledge and experience that the business will require and map out what you would do for yourself immediately.

    If you possess most of the skill-set and know-how required by the business, this can draw some advantages to the business if not, this could mean either setting time aside to familiarize with the new skill or the possibility of outsourcing the same to someone competent.

3) *Business Idea Validation* –Most business ideas are not well researched and thoroughly thought-through and this presents the problem of always thinking you have amazing ideas and it's human nature to always think you are right.

You could think that you have found a breakthrough to a common problem; however, it's always necessary to conduct research to find out if it will be successful. According to *Fortune* magazine, a recent investigative study on failed start-ups revealed that the **#1** reason that most businesses failed, cited lack of market need for the product and which also accounted for more than 42 per cent of the failed businesses.

This heightens the need to always validate the idea through solicitation of honest feedback, opinion and commentaries from possible would-be end users of the product or service before embarking on the establishing, building and money-spending phases. Widen the scope of your feedback by incorporating Face book, LinkedIn Groups, GrowthHackers, Reddit, ProductHunt etc.

4) *State your Competitive Advantage* –This defines the unique factors that set you apart from the rest and that allow you to generate more sales and customer retention over and above the other competitors. This is what makes your business stand out.

This could take the form of great product offering, distribution network, costing framework, amazing customer rapport and support centre mechanisms.

5) *Set SMART goals*– A short term goal is something you want to achieve in the near future which could be today, the coming week, this month or even this year. These are necessary when considering attainment of long term goals as it helps in breaking them down into bits or chunks referred to as milestones. Once attained, it gives a proud feeling of having done something worthwhile yet difficult as you work your way towards achieving the longer term goals. If the gratification of achieving a milestone is too far away, it becomes strenuous to be dedicated and stay steady to the cause.

At the start, your daily goals will be accomplishment of tasks on your to-do-list and eventually gravitate towards attaining some milestones as you near your business launching date.

6) *Direct your Master-plan Above & Beyond the Launch*–The ability to be a successful entrepreneur calls for proactive plans to guarantee business sustainability now and in the future, which is something no one else can do for you.

Adam Neumann, the co-founder of *WeWork* is a strong believer of, "Always know your plan-B." Problem-solving capabilities and walking your way around turbulent situations will determine your business prosperity.

7) *Outsource*–In the business establishment phase; outsource as much opportunities as possible.

This is the point; when you have made a proclamation that you are the leading social media and promotional marketing guru who is result oriented, your webpage, blog site as well as online persona should not look like a high school dropout developed it. Fixing the fonts, the colours, and make it match with the content will take some time of concerted learning, if not months and that's if you don't already possess the requisite knowledge to do all this, then it makes business sense to outsource such a service.

8) *Cross the line of Personal Projects and your Job at your own Peril*–Your contract fully stipulates the rules of engagement unless the employer missed out on some crucial content and pointers which is highly unlikely and it wouldn't amount to best practice and would be the opposite.

Here's the point; refrain from utilization of company materials, resources on your personal projects no matter how much the temptation flares. Steer away from your officially allocated computer or laptop, software, online application tools, help from colleagues at work etc.

Make consultations with your attorney on matters relating to non-disclosure agreements, assignment of invention clauses, or if you are under any non-compete clauses.

9) *Target the Mass Market before you Quit your Job*–It's important to validate the idea, take time to discover the available target market and getting feedback on the product response before going full-out on it.

It's a good habit to keep tabs with what is happening in your business world and seek advice from others. This practice alone will ensure your show of hits home with customers.

ii) **How to identify and leverage on your unique gifts to begin your business and attract the right clients for your business.**

Discover your Unique Gift: Personal Branding

To discover your unique gift and seek clarity with what makes you unique and what has helped many professionals to rekindle the flames of their passion, you will need to uncover the uniqueness and come up with a personal brand statement.

This process highlights your objective and leverages on your gifts and optimizes your influence on the globe. The clarity part is important as it helps you to attain your potential by reconfiguring your life around your God given gifts.

The Following Questions help to Figure out and Establish a Tie between You and Your Uniqueness;

1. What is it that you do with labouring and presents itself to you naturally?
2. What makes you exude with excitement and vitality?
3. What thing (1) would make you rise up early in the morning?
4. What would get you working even without the thought of compensation?
5. When are your happiest moments?

Reflect and consider the last time you posed these questions to yourself! The real test is why don't you ask yourself these questions more frequently?

What Makes your Business Unique?

What Factors Differentiate You from the Rest?

I will provide responses to the above two questions as we go along. There are hundreds of professionals in any given locality, be it a city or a county. There are also thousands of businesses that require the services of professionals and every one of them may require about 30-50 clients to create the business and vision that they have been dreaming of.

The truth of the matter is that, when we talk about basic services of a professional, they simply don't exist and this is the same for all professions be it audit and tax advice, banking and finance, real estate consultancy, legal consultancy, technology consultants etc. However, these are the most sought after services and providing these services like book keeping entails accuracy and ethical moral guidance to perform the duty to become a force to reckon with in the market.

The solution lies in *differentiation*; which is the experience levels executed and articulated by a businessperson to create a strong presence, create leverage and set them apart from the rest in a particular profession. Differentiation is established when a client experiences an outstanding and exceptional service. You are unique in your own right and there never will be anyone like you…your thoughts, actions, beliefs, contributions, talent cannot be replicated, therefore differentiation comes about in how you communicate and put your unique gifts to work.

"You will make an appalling somebody else, as you're the best "you" in existence. You are the unique person who can utilize your ability. It's an awesome responsibility"– **Anonymous**

iii) **Obstacles and How to Overcome them on your Journey to Prosperity**
Three of the most common obstacles that businesses face are;

1) Lack of capital.
2) Inadequate marketing strategy.
3) Restricted client base.

According to a research conducted by the *National Small Business Association (NSBA)*, 43 per cent of the businesses had inhibitions of capital access to execute their business plans into fruition; and 32 per cent were forced to lay their staff members redundant.

Because access to funding to get your business on its feet can be a vitiating element, why don't you attend to networking functions and explore the option of a possible investor?

52 per cent of businesses were culprits of not having a website; 70 per cent of those who had a site provided no means of advancing business with them; 68 per cent did not display contact of emails on their homepage landing; while 32 per cent did not have visible phone contacts. These are very disturbing figures for small businesses and so don't join this lot, as not having a website is being locked out of the rest of the world. Social media platforms can be a good head start with Face book, Instagram, LinkedIn and Twitter handles providing free marketing which could direct up to 75 per cent web traffic to your website.

9 Popular Business Obstacles and How to Overcome them

1. Use of Repetitive and Ineffectual Strategies.
   - Don't shy off from altering what's not possibly working.
   - Upgrade your systems and software packages.
   - Consider your exit strategy or make offers to your target clientele.

2. Exhaustion after Commission of an Error.
   - See difficulties as an opportunity to learn and excel.
   - Stay positive and shun away negativity.
   - View things on a much wider perspective.

3. Lost Motivation.
   - Look for motivational speakers and inspirational materials.
   - Cleanse your mind and take up a holiday.
   - Acquaint yourself with seminars/conferences for industry trends and updates.

4. Tunnel Vision Experiences.
   - Concentrate on long-term and have a vision for the business.
   - Establish new challenges & create goals and objectives to be attained.
   - Roister when you "shine."

5. Understaffed and Overworked?
   - Establish a dedicated team.
   - Delegate to team.
   - Hire trustworthy people.

6. Brand Identity Fading away.
   - Uphold your business integrity
   - Be consistent and persistent.
   - Don't forget, *how you do anything is how you do everything*.

7. Expand your Network.
   - Widen your scope of group network to deepen the contact list.
   - Enlist in an investment group in the locale.
   - Participate in community activities.

8. Losing Grip of Industry Trends?
   - Self-educate with good reads.
   - Be updated on the competition.
   - Follow the global economy and be attentive to the stock market.

9. Falling Short of Capital!
   - Regular budget reviews.
   - Communiqué with present clients on improvements.
   - Seek potential investors.

iv) **A Wealth of Success Tips and Guidelines that will Gravitate you towards Accomplishing your Desired Goal.**

12 Simple Money Habits You Can Start Today to Build Real Wealth

Becoming proficient with your money could mean adopting a few smart money habits.

According to Tom C. Corley an avid researcher on the wealthy and self-made millionaires and author of *Change Your Habits, Change Your Life*, he inscribes the following, "habits are the cause of wealth, poverty, happiness, sadness, stress, good relationships, bad relationships, good health, or bad health,"

The habits to embrace to get well-paid being successful, worthwhile, productive, profitable and money-making are as herein below;

1) *Automate your Personal Finances*–If you spend above an hour a week in managing your personal finances, then that's way too long. You need to automate your finances to your investment and savings accounts to allow you to focus on the bigger picture and build wealth smoothly as depicted by David Back, a self-made millionaire in his book *The Automatic Millionaire*.

    Simply link your accounts so your pay check goes unswerving and directly to your retirement or 401(k) plan, and savings accounts; and that can guarantee you won't fail in your wealth building efforts.

2) *Invest any Spare Money* –Contrary to common belief, you could start investing with the very little extra money that you receive that doesn't have immediate use.

    Take home from this is that; the sooner you begin investing, the earlier you could begin taking advantage of compounded interest. David Bach spells it out, "the miracle of compounding can transform a relatively small amount but consistent amounts of saving into major wealth."

3) *Axe the small Daily Purchases: Coffee, Energy bars, Nuts* –Bach formulated the term "The Latte Factor" the ideology was doing away with daily latte at a cost of US$5 a day which could amount to significant savings over a long period of time.

    US$5 per day for the daily coffee translates to US$150 a month. Bach reports, "If you invested US$150 a month and earned 10 per cent annual return, you would wind up with US$948,611 in 40 years."

We are all guilty of throwing away our money earned through merit on whimsical spending on small pleasures without realizing how much this could build up to.

4) *Invent and find Specific Money Goals–* From the authority of *Secrets of the Millionaire Mind* by self-made millionaire T. Harv Eker he unravels, "the number one reason people don't get what they want is that, they don't know what they want." He goes on to say, "Rich people are totally clear that they want wealth."

To get to the level of being clear he proposes jotting down goals on wealth and yearly earnings and at the very minimum love yourself enough to make it sensible and truthful.

5) *Don't Squander Unexpected Money Flows or Wind fall Gains–* Imagine that extra cash such as bonus pay, surprise money on an anniversary and any windfall gains as though they are non-existent.

Get such money to work for you by applying it to clear some existing debt or by channelling this directly into an investment account. Beginning this habit early will be beneficial since you will have developed in-built financial muscles to resist lifestyle inflation when you receive a large unexpected payout of money or a sudden rise in earnings.

6) *Act Rich, Emulate the Rich & You'll be Rich–* The typical income earner remains average because of their expectations, "The masses think they aren't worthy of great wealth. "Who am I, they ask themselves, to become a millionaire?" as Steve Siebold elucidates, the author of *How Rich People Think*. The rich people have this belief that "success, fulfillment and happiness are the natural order of existence." Siebold goes on to elaborate further, "This single belief drives the great ones to behave in ways that virtually guarantee their success."

7) *The Magic of Reading 30 Minutes a day–* Wealthy individuals have inclination to read and continuously invest in themselves even long after formative schooling days. Siebold commits to paper, "Walk into a wealthy person's home and one of the things you'll see is an extensive library of books they've used to educate themselves on how to become more successful."

If this formula has worked for self-made millionaires and billionaires, it could work out for you too, why don't you give it a try?

8) *Rich People Rise up Early–* Most wealthy people are predisposed to waking up early. Apple CEO, Tim Cook begins his morning at 3:45AM. Oprah Winfrey, Michelle Obama & Pepsi CEO, Indra Nooyi are known to wake up at the crack of first light. Twitter co-founder Jack Dorsey and Virgin Group founder Richard Branson form part of

the respectable 5:00AM club and these are not the only prosperous people who wake up before day break.

Tom C. Corley who has intensively researched hundreds of self-made millionaires in a 5 year study established that, almost 50 per cent of them rise up early at the minimum three-hours before their working day begins.

Waking up early isn't a guarantee that you will automatically become wealthy, but at least you will get more work done without a shadow of doubt.

9) *Embrace Yourself with Top-Performers–* Do not ever for once underestimate the might, power and influence of those you surround yourself with. Matter-of-factly, your wealth has inclination to mirror your closest of allies and accomplices.

Siebold, the self-made millionaire puts it in black and white, "We become like the people we associate with, and that's why winners are attracted to winners." He goes on to say, "Successful people generally agree that consciousness is contagious, and that exposure to people who are more successful has the potential to expand your thinking and catapult your income"

10) *Keep Track of your Spending Patterns–* You can't build wealth when you don't have a clue of what comes in and what goes out. Just to be sure you are making more than you are spending it becomes sensible to track your daily expenditure.

You could do this easily by use of a spreadsheet on your laptop or desktop computer or utilize a few apps such as *Personal Capital* and *Mint* from the comfort of your phone.

11) *Magnify your 401(k) or Pension Contributions–* The more you make reservations and allocate towards this cause, the better but as a conservative estimate contribute as much to qualify for the full employer match, this is basically costless and free-money.

Thereafter, work on swelling your contributions regularly either half-yearly or annually whenever you receive either a gratuity payment or pay increase.

12) *Being Comfortable with Discomfort brings Growth–* Getting out of your comfort zone will bring the much desired earnings and growth in most spheres of life.

Though the majority don't push for a pay rise, it doesn't hurt to shoot for it since those who make requests end up receiving it after all. And this difference in earning can spell out the divergence between an ordinary life and that of a highly-paid worker.

As self-made millionaire Grant Sabatier puts it, "The number one thing that will dictate your future earning potential and get you to US$1 million the fastest is how much money you are being paid today."

Ultimate Thoughts:

As per the revelations afore-mentioned from the *National Small Business Association (NSBA)*, I reiterate, 43 per cent of businesses fail as a result of capital inadequacies. Moreover, not unless you are diligently working on a rapid-organic growth start-up, and can access ready investor-funding or own-funding, you may practically and realistically have to get some form of sustenance income before the new project kicks-off in a big-way and is able to support both you and the business.

Commencing a business while in full-time employment can be quite taxing. Nonetheless, it's conceivable and possible.

CHAPTER 5

Investing in Stock Could Make you a Millionaire

*"I will tell you how to become rich. Close the doors; be fearful when others are greedy. Be greedy when others are fearful"- **Warren Buffett, CEO & Chairman, Berkshire Hathaway Inc.***

The 7 Warren Buffet Stock Investing Secrets

Warren Buffett is plausibly one of the greatest investors of all time. From the authority of Robert G. Hagstrom in his explorative series on Buffett's investment principles entitled *The Warren Buffett Way*, of the 69 people who featured in the 1993 *Forbes* list, Buffett was the only one who had an accumulated wealth of about US$8.3 billion from trading in the stock market alone.

If you want to be a stock market millionaire the greatest favour you could do yourself, is to talk to a stock market millionaire - Buffett is a billionaire in that case. Attendees of annual Berkshire Hathaway meetings get blessings of astuteness and nuggets of his investing wisdom which is tantamount to receiving costless money.

Buffett is an avid preacher of value investing – choosing to be guided by the companies operating results and not by short term market fluctuations – in which he selects stock prices of companies that have been undervalued.

1) A Recipe to Stay Sane while others are Going Berserk

Buffett explains that the typical investor should expect four-five economic crises in their lifetime. The point here is; to have what it takes to exploit them to the max, so far the dot-com and the housing bubble bursts having gone past, it means there could be two-three more to come.

This in essence means when the market comes crashing, you need the intellectual capacity to stay in the game until such a time that you dispose of the losses (or gains) as they are just but theoretical and only appear on paper. Even when your retirement or 401(k) statement indicates a loss of US$8,000 the previous quarter, that's just on paper. Gather the mental toughness to keep the investment so that you could earn a higher return above the typical investor.

This is an indication that you have to keep investing more money when the market is falling. It could appear counter instinctive, but this is the reasoning: assume stock to be foodstuffs, when the prices fall, this is equated to them being on sale and automatically everybody would tend to stock up. In the same vein, buy stock when market prices have plummeted. Once you grasp this concept, upon prices falling, you won't let your emotions take over and make you do something dumb!

"Following those rules, the 'know nothing' investor who both diversifies and keeps his cost minimal is virtually certain to get satisfactory results," Buffett inscribes. "Accumulate shares over a long-period, and never sell when the news is bad and stocks are well of their highs."

2) Stick to Your Area of Expertise

Buffett's advice to investors who have little or no time to research on stock is to adhere to low-cost index funds or mutual funds. Buffett would skip stock whose basics appear rather complex to comprehend. Matter-of-factly, Buffett has specifically left his wife instructions in his will to the effect that the trust should channel 90 per cent in low index funds or mutual funds and 10 per cent towards short-term government bonds.

Financial and stock analysts on full-time employment make investment guidance and provide direction and still have a 50-50 chance of getting the stock prediction wrong or right.

What makes you think you who devotes a few hours on the weekend stand a better chance of picking the right stock? The probability is low. Choice of individual securities cannot be equated to being a predictor of future stock performance.

3) **Ignore Economic Forecasts – They're Usually Wrong**

Absolutely no one knows the direction the economy will take including POTUS, the most powerful person in the world and even Buffett himself; therefore it's an exercise in futility to base your investment decisions on forecasts.

Most of the 24-hour business channels discuss forecasts on the economy extensively cynically; the stock market is an early indicator which means it can turn out of a bear market before the economy shows any signals of a recovery. Similarly, the same situation applies to a recession. You should embark and abide by a solid long-term investment plan instead of relying on economic trends. It may not be a smooth ride all the way but, it's the way leading to your goal.

4) **Know Your Limits**

Buffett advises investors and future business leaders to stick to what they know in tough times and they will succeed. "You don't need to be an expert in order to achieve satisfactory investment returns." Buffett was quoted talking to his shareholders. "But if you aren't, you must recognize your limitations and follow a course certain to work reasonably well."

To drive his point home, Buffett explained two investments that he made in real estate. A commercial building in New York University (NYU), not being an expert in property management and a farm in Nebraska, and not conversant in farming he nonetheless expected to succeed for the simple reason, farmers would continue to grow corn in Nebraska and NYU student population numbers will notwithstanding continue to swell.

5) **Future Productivity should be your Cornerstone**

Buffett has a straight-forward philosophy: Purchase investments that will generate good value in the long-haul and acquire them at a reasonable price. Buffett champions for investors to put more focus on the future assets productivity than buying stock on the basis of market predictions or past performance. Buffett and his investing partner Charlie Munger begin by making convincing and compelling estimates of what the companies expect to earn 5 years ahead of time before arriving at a purchase decision for stock.

Upon making estimates of earnings 5 years away and 5 years into the future and the yield looks promising, they then examine the stock price. If the selling price is reasonable in comparison to the bottom boundary of the estimate of earnings, then they can enter into a decision to purchase the stock and keep it. Buffett says when they are unable to make a compelling earnings estimate they get on to the next one.

It's thought-provoking to note that Buffett restricts himself to placing bets on productivity of companies' assets of American descent and is not too bothered on what looms on the international scenes, even in difficult times of financial depression.

6) **Keep off Price Speculation**

Buffett seriously warns against possibly timing prices against market oscillations. He goes on further to explain that, though there's nothing wrong with price speculation, but very few people possess this expertise. "Half of all coin-flippers will win their first toss," retorts Buffett. "None of those winners has an expectation of profit if he continues to play the game." People are expectant to make great gains, but are seldomly honest when it comes to when they stand to gain in the long-term speculation.

If you enjoy the thrill of speculation, set to one side a tiny proportion of your portfolio to suit trading intents. The flipside is acquiring value investments at the earliest opportunity and you don't have to wait for the bottoming out of the market.

7) **Rely on Productive & Efficient companies, Not Pundits**

Too many investors listen to investment pundits and the so-called "investment experts" to try and land on large windfall gains. Buffett does the reverse by consciously investing in well-managed businesses and at an opportune-time rather than timing the market upswings.

"When I hear TV commentators glibly opine on what the market will do next," Buffett inscribed, "I am reminded of Mickey's Mantle's scathing comment: 'You don't know how easy this game is until you get into that broadcasting booth.'" In a nutshell, don't be guided by the pundit's presumptions on the market swings in your investment decisions. Wise decisions arrive at sound investments which over the long-haul are not affected by the movements in the economic development, interest rates and short-term stock market sways.

Revealed: How to Become a Stock Market Millionaire

Becoming a stock market millionaire is much easier that you ever thought. Once you have put down a robust foundation and made things automated, all you have to do is sit back and relax and watch your money grow.

At the first opportunity you will need to spare about two hours of your precious time to get started and this will guarantee you more than 90 per cent likelihood of turning into a stock millionaire.

Setting a foundation means devising a working strategy, as you cannot be hopping-in and out trying to select the most appropriate time to buy and sell and also following up on returns. It's of paramount importance to adopt a strategy and adhere to it in both good and bad times.

Below herein is an *Easy-to-Follow Guide* that will help you build tremendous wealth in the stock market.

Become A Millionaire Trading on Stocks: *An Easy-to-follow Guide*

Revelation #1: Devise a Plan
Revelation #2: Set up an Account
Revelation #3: Automate your Transfers
Revelation #4: Select Low-cost Investments
Revelation #5: Diversify
Revelation #6: Avoid pursuing Returns, Remain Invested
Revelation #7: Monitor Progress towards your Goals

Become A Millionaire Trading on Stocks: *An Easy-to-follow Guide*

Revelation #1: Devise a Plan

You will struggle without a plan both in life and in investments. This is equivalent to beginning a journey without the end-of-the-line in mind. What do you carry in your luggage? Which route will you use? How do you know you have arrived at your destination? Ideally, you begin with the *end* in mind. The same can be said of investing achievements. Putting down goals in written form of a plan compels you to figure out the end results and exactly what is to be done in between.

On the authority of Jon Dulin the author of *"Seven Easy Steps to Early Retirement,"* planning is very critical in investments. For most investors who move from investment to the next one and therefore don't afford time for their portfolio to grow, they tend to have this notion that the stock market is rigged against them.

What actually works against these investors is lack of a plan, which is the reason for their unsuccessful stock investments.

A plan ensures ability to gauge if you have achieved your investment goals, and if you have veered of the target, it can help you to change course and get back on track.

Below herein are some questions which should come to mind and that you should factor in when putting up an investment plan;

1) *Why the interest in the Investment?*–the first question that comes to mind is why are you putting your money in an investment. Is it for children's future education, a wedding, retirement, a car, a house, a farm?

2) *Time Horizon?*–The length of time the investment is made and held before being liquidated. In short after how long would the invested money be required? Retirement should be long-term 30-40 years but very much dependant on the investor's age at the time of making the investment, while holiday or acquisition of an automobile is short term and can be attainable within a short span of time.

    The unwritten rule is generally that any investment with goals beyond 5 years should be invested in stock, while for shorter goals should be invested in bonds, COD's and savings accounts.

3) *Levels of Risk Tolerance*–When the goal is clear including when the money will be needed, the next thing is to think of how to invest and as a norm anything upwards of 5 years should be invested in stocks. But one more honest answer to yourself would be what proportion of the portfolio should be directed towards stocks.

    The allocation agreed upon should strike a balance between being both towards achievement of your goal and it being comfortable enough to allow you to get some decent sleep in the night. *To be precise: Take Consideration of the Amount of Money you stand to Gain versus the Amount of Money you Could Loose.* Taking a much higher risk would mean more money to be earned but weigh it in against how awful you would feel if you lost the money instead.

    If 60 per cent of your money invested in stock is considered risky, it's worth lowering it to 40 per cent and 60 per cent in bonds but this could be against the backdrop of your goal taking longer to be achieved, as bonds don't attract as much earnings. If you are in your youthful ages it won't make sense going beneath this risk threshold.

4) *How Much Funds are Required*– You will need to know the amount of money required in order to determine how much to be mobilized towards the savings. For a car, house or a holiday away it's rather straight-forward and the amounts can easily be figured-out.

But for pension it gets a bit more complicated. Here's how to arrive at an estimation that will guide you on how much to put towards your savings plan:

i) Tabulate how much your expenditure will amount to in a month.
ii) To arrive on the annual expenditure (cast this for the 12 months).
iii) You require the retirement in 30 years' time (**x** 30 years).

The figure that you arrive at is the amount of funds required at the age of retirement. If your expenditure amounts to US$3,000 per month, this tabulated over a year is US$36,000. The amount you will therefore need to afford a comfortable retirement is US$1,080,000.

Some expenses will not be there during retirement while others will crop in old age; nevertheless, this is a reliable estimate by all standards.

5) *How Much of Your Income Should You Save?* – Upon establishing the amount to save, you will need to work out the monthly savings. You still have time to make things work, so don't be hard on yourself if you're not able to mobilize sufficient monthly savings towards your intended goal.

This is where a budget comes in handy. By keeping records of all expenditures you will be able to note where to cut expenses which will have an effect of improving the savings channelled towards your goals. For example unnecessary spending out on dinners could be reduced and the funds directed towards the savings account, which become very apparent when you introduce a budget to monitor items money is spent on.

It's prudent to work on the big expenditure items before embarking on the small items like the mortgage repayment and motor insurance; look for possible avenues of reducing the outgoing costs by probably refinancing the mortgage and shopping for better and cheaper insurance and the savings mobilized could be put towards your investment.

For long-term goals like retirement, it's always safe to save a percentage for instance like 15-20 per cent while for shorter-term goals this could work out by splitting the expenditure over the period it would be required. For example raising US$30,000 over 5 years for deposit for a house works out to US$500 per month in form of savings.

However, always remember there's a higher propensity to make more money than cutting back on expenses.

The need to have an investment plan is so that you don't pick up investments haphazardly and hope all will be well towards the finishing line. You have to know why the investment is critical and write down specific answers in response to this question. Identifying your goals early helps in directing money towards where it makes a lot more sense and position yourself in a way that will make your goals attainable.

Revelation #2: Set up an Account

This is a normal exercise and you can always contact your broker to advice on the type of investments accounts that are available in the market. However, there are plenty of options when it comes to opening of investments accounts and I would strongly recommend the following;

Investment Account	Limit (US$)
M1 Finance	Up to 1,000 and more than 1,000
Betterment	Up to 1,000 and more than 1,000
Schwab	Less than 10,000
Vanguard	More than 10,000

Revelation #3: Automate your Transfers

Setting up a recurring payment on a monthly basis to your investment account would be the next important step or consult your broker to advice more on the same. Frequent investing in the stock market is a *necessary* and *sufficient* condition to turn into a stock market millionaire and this can't happen on an ad-hoc investing basis.

Investing US$1 and waiting for it to become US$1 million would not be prudent and could be a long wait of 173 years. However, if you invested US$100 at an annual growth at the same rate of 8 per cent the time will be cut down drastically to 53 years.

Look at how the following scenario's play out;

	Amount to Invest per month (in US$)	Annual Rate of Return (ROR per cent)	# of years to become a Stock Millionaire
Scenario 1	US$1	8 %	173
Scenario 2	US$100	8 %	53

The secret is how to become a stock millionaire in less than the laid down 30 years. And here's how to do it; save only US$667 per month and direct it towards your stock investment.

Below herein is the work out:

	Annual Salary (US$)	10% into 401(k) or retirement	Subtract from US$8,004 (US$667 x 12)	Divide by 12 -Additional amount to save to be Millionaire @ Age 30
Scenario 1	35,000	3,500	4,504	375
Scenario 2	60,000	6,000	2,004	167

Illustration of Stock Investment by Age 30

The figures in grey indicate that the goal of being a millionaire by age 30 is feasible if you devote to saving 15-20 per cent of your income and direct it to your stock investment.

	Monthly Commitment in US$ to Inject to turn Millionaire @:								
	Age 30	Age 35	Age 40	Age 45	Age 50	Age 55	Age 60	Age 65	Age 70
18	4,146	2,313	1,396	875	563	367	242	160	106
20	5,458	2,875	1,688	1,063	667	433	283	188	125
25	13,500	5,458	2,875	1,688	1,063	667	433	283	188
30		13,500	5,458	2,875	1,688	1,063	667	433	283
35			13,500	5,458	2,875	1,688	1,063	667	433
40				13,500	5,458	2,875	1,688	1,063	667
45					13,500	5,458	2,875	1,688	1,063
50						13,500	5,458	2,875	1,688
55							13,500	5,458	2,875
60								13,500	5,458
65									13,500

Take away from Step #3: It's better to suffer now by mobilizing more savings than enjoy now only to realize it in your old age that you don't have enough saved up and get forced to work into your sunset years. The more the savings the quicker you realize your dream of being a stock millionaire.

Revelation #4: Select Low-cost Investments

For every mutual fund that you place your investment in there is always a management fee payable. The rate of return (ROR), displayed on your statement is shown net of the fees. For example if the management fee was 1 per cent and your ROR on the statement was indicated as 7 per cent, essentially this means the investment ROR was 8 per cent.

What is Considered a Low Management Fee?

Essentially you shouldn't pay more than 1 per cent as fees under all circumstances.

Many investors make this grotesque misconception that a higher fee could mean expertise of the fund manager in their field of endeavour and ability to earn you more returns. This is actually further from the truth, just like a laundry that charges a premium rate of about $2 above the others, it would be wrong to assume there would be more value addition in provision of their services. More people would have inclination to choose the premier service provider over the competitors presuming there would be more value addition. This is the same mistake people make in investments and loose what should have formed part of their investment.

Opting for a low-cost investment could have implications that are twofold:

i) You achieve your millionaire goal much quicker.
ii) You also end up with more money in your investment.

Illustration 1: John Rose invested his savings of US$1,000 in stock trading through Company A, a mutual fund manager over a 30 years period with a management fee of 1.25 per cent that returned earnings of 8 per cent per annum. Later on, he stumbled onto Company B which in contrast charged a lower management fee of 0.30 per cent annually.

In 30 years John Rose would have paid US$1,200 in fees while if he would have done a bit more of his homework earlier and invested in Company B he would have actually paid US$850 lower in fees.

It's easy to take this amount for granted. But this amount compounded over the 30 years period is a substantial amount of money.

Management fee	Invested Amount (in US$)	Annual Rate of Return (ROR percent)	Investment after 30 years
Company A (1.25%)	US$850	8 %	US$7,096
Company B (0.03%)	US$850	8 %	US$9,257

The US$850 in fees evidently builds up to slightly over US$2,000 over the 30 years period.

Note that the more the investment, the more the fees increase.

Illustration 1: If John Rose invested US$50,000 the payable fees at 1.25 per cent management fees would have been US$60,000 over the 30 years period while if he had in a fund that applied a management fee of 0.03 per cent the fees would have been US$17,000.

By going for an investment with a lower fee he would in essence have more than US$100,000 in savings

Management fee	Invested Amount (in US$)	Annual Rate of Return (ROR percent)	Investment after 30 years
Company A (1.25%)	US$50,000	8 %	US$354,818
Company B (0.03%)	US$50,000	8 %	US$462,850

Revelation #5: Diversify

According to *The Balance,* investing transfers a certain amount of risk which could either occasion pain or gain. Remember the adage, "No pain, no gain?

For any type of investment it's important to weigh the latent risk against the reward to arrive at a decision whether it's a worthwhile decision. Comprehending the relationship between risk and reward is the underlying factor in establishing personal investments principles and beliefs.

In a good year stocks could earn 51 per cent and get as low as 37 per cent while bonds could attract a high of 17 per cent and a low of 11 per cent. Investment like mutual funds (low-index funds), bonds and stocks also carry their own risk profile and comprehending the differences will go a long way in assisting you to diversify and safeguard your portfolio.

If you were to create a diversified portfolio of 50 per cent bonds and 50 per cent stocks the latent gains shifts to 32 per cent gain while the latent loss dips to a gain of -17 per cent. Spun over a period of 15-20 years the numbers even out and the returns show marked improvements.

This could also mean investments in all forms of shares – growth or value, small cap, large cap, international or local - and for bond could be either investment in - short-term, long-term, government, corporate and even junk bonds.

The importance of diversification is to empower you to earn the greatest rewards while shouldering the lowest amount of risk, therefore there is power in getting the right mix of investments.

How could you possibly go about making adjustments to improve and get to your ultimate mix of an investment portfolio, how would you know if you are too diversified or under-diversified in your current circumstances?

There are two alternatives: automated and manual

i) *Automated Alternative: Personal Capital* – This entails establishing a free account and tie-up your investments. It will plot a figure that displays your present portfolio by percentages. In a short moment you are able to know what actions to take to enter into diversification. It also offers other advantages such as a free retirement planner and fee scrutiny.

ii) *Manual Alternative* – This is best executed using MS Excel spreadsheet. The greatest advantage of taking this option is the ability to take control over the portfolio and how you want it to work for you, only that you will have to keep making the amendments and refreshing.

Revelation #6: Avoid Pursuing Returns, Remain Invested

Pursuing returns is one of the reasons the typical investors earns returns as low as 2 per cent.

Reasons why chasing returns doesn't work:

1) It has the effect of increasing the costs payable on trading fees and commissions
2) The investment resolutions are based on past performance which isn't a predictor of what returns would be made in the future.

In the long-haul it's widely accepted that movement of the market is positive and will rise upwards over time. After the *dot.com* crisis the markets recovered 260 per cent from when it had dipped the most in 2009. If an investor remained invested they would have even recovered from the losses of the crash as evidently the strongest bull markets were experienced though a good number of investors fled never to return to the stock markets after the collapse of the stock market of 2008. Below is the Dow-Jones chart, it shows an inclination of the market to be positive overall and any investment chart will depict this trend.

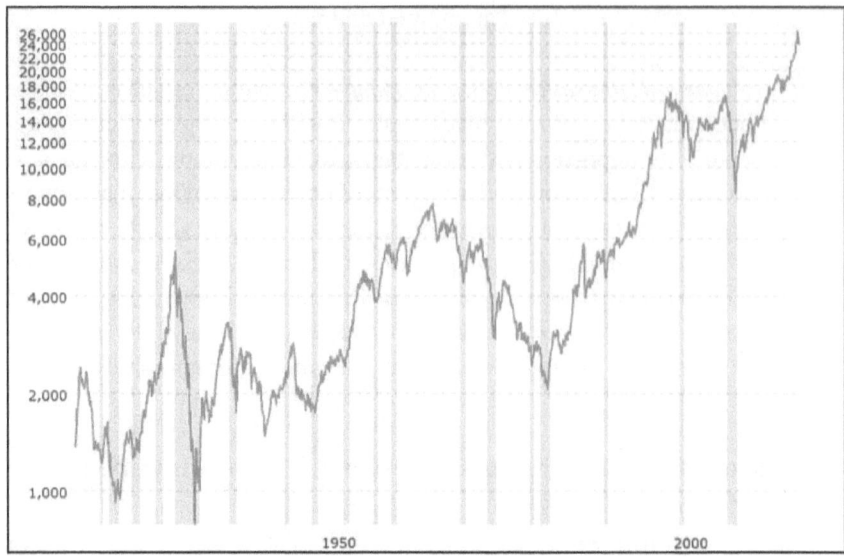

The Dow-Jones Chart

In order to be a stock millionaire *greed* and *fear* become two of your worst enemies and that you will have to take control of. You will have to desist from watching TV, limit reads online, in magazines and periodicals. Keep in mind the bourse all over the world is left open to enable you to trade and therefore the more trades, the more there is money to be made by all parties.

Revelation #7: Monitor Progress towards your Goals

It's important to monitor progress to know if you are on course to attaining your long term-goals. *Personal Capital* offers the best option to scrutinize your portfolio by giving a percentage breakdown, the most up to date balances as well as fees payable for all your investments.

If for example your ultimate portfolio mix is 60 per cent stock and 40 per cent bonds, and at the year-end an analysis reveals that it stands at 68 per cent stocks and 32 per cent bonds it means you will have to rebalance by selling of 8 per cent of stocks and use the revenue generated to acquire more bonds.

Interpretation of the rebalancing act: this has to be done in order to stay on course to attaining your goal as bonds tend to give lower earnings than stocks. When your investment portfolio is composed of more stocks than bonds it means you are presuming a higher risk than you are at ease with and therefore a need to take the remedial action to stay on course.

Guiding Principles for rebalancing:

i) Review your portfolio twice a year – mid-year and at the year-end.
ii) Only rebalance stock that is way-off by 5 per cent or more. If the ultimate portfolio mix is 60/40 and analyzed result discloses 64/36, don't be too bothered.
iii) For portfolios which the buying and selling attracts taxes, it's prudent to buy more of the portfolio required to balance the mix so that all the new money that flows in, is directed towards the purchase of this investment. For example, if the ultimate portfolio mix is 60/40 and you have 80 per cent in stocks and 20 per cent in bonds, all the funds flowing in should be towards purchase of bonds until such a time that the mix is arrived at.

Ultimate Thoughts:

This seems like a lot of information to take in at one go. The easiest way to get started is by selecting your goals and settling for the monthly outgoing towards the savings account, the rest of the things will fall into place along the process.

If you embark on these *Easy-to-Follow* steps you will well be on your way to becoming a stock market millionaire joining the ranks of Warren Buffett who is worth $84 billion (March 6, 2019) and David Ohana, KenolKobil's CEO who exited the helm of the company, having made a profit of US$11 million from sale of his employee share option plan, (ESOP) stake to French Multinational Rubis Energie in a recent buyout of the oil marketer according to *Business Daily* of April 12, 2019.

Gideon Muriuki, CEO, Co-operative Bank of Kenya also earned a dividend of slightly over US$1 million according to *Business Daily* of March 24, 2019 from his 1.77 per cent stake in the bank.

CHAPTER 6

Do Less and Make More OPM, OPT, OPW, OPI, OPE

"Your workforce is your most valued asset. The knowledge and skills they have represent the fuel that drives the engine of business, and you can leverage on that knowledge"- **Harvey Mackay**

On the authority of Tony Robbins;

92 per cent of the 17 million that try to quit smoking fail.
95 per cent of people who loose weight fail to keep it long-term.
88 per cent of people who set New Year's resolution fail at their attempts.

Only 10 per cent of the population has specific, well-defined goals, but even then, seven out of ten of those people reach their goals only 50 per cent of the time.

The greatest artillery that can also be the largest impediment towards creating change is; *Power of Leverage.*

Change is a function of motivation and not capability. If we took change to be a "should", you wouldn't expect people to take up change positively. Change has got to be a MUST and for it to have long lasting effects; there has got to be some form of commitments.

It becomes necessary to associate PAIN with not changing right now, and **leverage on great PLEASURE now for making instantaneous change** and link it to a new pattern of behaviour that will make it a permanent change and that will gravitate you ultimately to success.

Power of Leverage

One of the most powerful weapons known to the wealthy is the term "leverage." Leverage to them means to do more with less. The wealthy have for a long-time known that the most influential master plan and blueprint to attain phenomenal wealth and wield power and authority is to leverage on your own money, resources, time, skills and consolidate with leveraging on other people's money, time, resources and skills.

Robert Kiyosaki had this to say; "leverage is the reason some people become rich and others do not." According to Tony Robbins author of the eBook *Power of Leverage*, the leverage concept possesses the influence to provide you with more time, greater fitness, financial control, career success, business prosperity as well as satisfaction in a relationship. According to me leverage is not only about creation of wealth; it's more of establishing freedom so I can do more of what I enjoy doing the most and with the people I care about.

But What is Leverage Anyway?

According to Brad Sugars the author of 14 business books including *"The Business Coach", "Instant Cash Flow"* and *"Billionaire in Training"* leverage is a concept of achieving ever more with ever less that you have to fully comprehend and which is a pivotal tool for success in business.

A common delusion is that leverage applies to borrowing finances because it's most commonly referred to in discussions about financial concepts like debt, financing and investments. People who own large housing estates know how to use the bank's facilities by pledging a proportion of the cash they own (usually 10-20 per cent) and taking advantage of the power of leverage to get financed the difference using other people's money and still gain 100 per cent control over the ownership of expansive parcels of properties.

This concept can be applied beyond debt, financing and investment as was featured in a *Forbes* article, "10 Powerful Women Who Played Team Sports." *Forbes* went on to write;

> "–Irene Rosenfield, Chairman Kraft Foods
> –Mary Schapiro, Chairman of the Securities and Exchange Commission
> –Ellen Kullman, CEO of DuPont
>
> ...and more all leveraged their time on the basket court, lacrosse field and more to learn critical lessons about teamwork, tenacity, success and failure. In other words, they did more with their experience than become better athletes and win games. They internalized how to make a team run, how to come back after defeat and how to work diligently to achieve success. They got ahead in their respective fields because they transferred athletic training concepts to their workplace and, eventually, the chairman's office. Whether or not you played sports growing up, you can leverage different aspects of your life to your professional advantage."

The concept of leverage is all about using less to achieve more. It entails making your teams achieve more using less effort, it's getting your advertising and promotional campaigns to return much more sales than the dollars spent on the cost; it's all about getting impressive results while utilizing much more less, time after time.

Time happens to be one of the most valuable resources in the world today. If you lost money you could always make up for it, but time loss is never recoverable.

It comes as no surprise that John D. Rockefeller an American business magnate, industrialist and philanthropist who is also considered the wealthiest American of all time understood the power of leverage and once stated.

> *"I would rather earn 1% off a 100 people's efforts than 100 % of my own efforts"*- **John D. Rockefeller**

If you are on a day job you realize that time is your most valuable resource and being an employee doesn't offer you that luxury and in fact, gives you little or no leverage at all on your time which I can tell you for free is not a SMART thing to do.

I'm Self-Employed, isn't this Optimal Leverage?

Being in self-employment – A doctor practicing by himself, an accountant or lawyer, small business entrepreneur, real estate agent managing your own office and running your own business, you could be very pressed for time and have even less leverage than a typical employee would.

More often than not, you have to run with all aspects of the business - client visitations, giving the business direction, business development, marketing, closing the sale, jostling between product purchase, the logistics until delivery point, performing accounting functions and chasing debts. The odds are that the typical employee is far much better off as you could be putting in longer hours and the saddest part is that you don't get paid when you are not working and don't have paid holidays or even days off.

If you found yourself in such a tricky situation, word of advice is go back to the drawing board, and re-think how you could leverage on your time so that you could have your life back and enjoy more freedom.

Big doors swing on little hinges and in the business world how well you learn to apply the power of leverage on your time will determine how much freedom you can have in your life. For me, I have so far written 20 books. I only have to write them once and by leveraging on them, I get paid for the rest of my life.

Forms of Leverage

i) **OPM (Other People's Money)** - Allows you to acquire assets quicker and command a large stake than saving such an amount would, as it could take a considerable amount of time and the purchasing power could be eroded by inflation over the years. A good example is investing in real estate. It gives you capability to construct rental apartments by putting down a deposit of 10-20 per cent and leverage on other people's money (the banks) and get financed 80-90 per cent of the project cost. This presents an opportunity to have paying tenants whose rental payments are directed towards the monthly outgoing mortgage instalment repayments and you keep the difference to yourself and still end up controlling 100 per cent of the property. The beauty of this is that it gets constructed once and for the rest of its useful life it will pay you both rental income and appreciate in terms of capital growth. Other examples of OPM – Fund raising by direct solicitation for funds from investors for execution of a viable business idea or completion of a development project for a share in the profits generated, a refined and worldly-wise incurs a debt from a broker to do margin trading.

ii) **OPT (Other People's Time)** – Individuals will sell you their time, talent, know-how, connections and resources at a comparatively cheap price or could in certain circumstances volunteer it free of charge. Companies buy time in the form of specialization taken up by professionals with special skills as well as labourers. Hiring all these professionals such as lawyers, accountants, realtors, and actuaries allows utilization of their skills and knowledge while at the same time freeing up time to make additional income from other multiple sources of income (MSI's). Other examples of OPT – A financial advisor provides support and training to the new recruits and gets a percentage of their monthly production, a lady hires a weekend cleaner to dedicate more time at the weekend with the family, a networking guru provides support and training to her down line distributors and books a percentage of the distribution income they generate, an entrepreneur in New York hires the services of a virtual assistant in Nepal to continue billing clients as he gets rest for the night.

iii) **OPW (Other People's Work)** – Bears similarities with OPT but you instead hire people to leverage on their time. Most people are in desperate need of security rather than opportunity and that's why most people find jobs. Hire and delegate everything to them that you can't do as well or you just don't want to do. Bill Gates applies this principle widely and is able to effectively leverage on time, ability and energy of almost 70,000 employees. This explains why at the end of every year Bill Gates still emerges top as one of *The Richest Men in the World*, yet at the beginning of the year we all have a similar allocation of time available which is 8,760 hours or 525,600 minutes in our time bank. He has perfected the art of utilising OPW to his own credit.

iv) **OPI (Other People's Ideas)** – This alludes to association with people who can share and replicate great revenue generating ideas. Businesses utilizing networks and franchises' are existing proof of OPI at work. The basics of wealth creation never change; it rests entirely on leveraging on OPI. A good example is when a business magnate acquires a popular restaurant franchise - McDonald's, Subway, Wendy's, Domino's Pizza, Pizza Hut, Burger King or KFC.

v) **OPE (Other People's Experiences)** - It's a complete waste of time to relearn what other people have known and perfected over the years. The best way to tap into OPE is through learned experiences, expertise, as well as flaws and faults of others. Common examples would take the form of colleges, universities, audios, seminars and podcasts. The simplest way to get rich is to personally apprentice with a rich person, learn what they know, meet up their contacts and replicate what they do – or do it even better or even read the books written by the rich. For example read *"Rich Dad Poor Dad"* by Robert Kiyosaki and practice the concepts therein, you will nonetheless, become rich. Other great examples of OPE – Retaining the services of an accomplished attorney, tax advisors, real estate agent in your team when embarking on real estate projects, consultations with a medical surgeon for a complicated surgery, receiving value investing lessons from a stock-savvy mentor to learn the art of expert stock trading, establishing a marketing network through replicating efforts of a successful up line principal whose already made it, taking part in a mastermind class to network with the well-to-do individuals and that you share similar goals and ambitions.

You could drastically reduce your learning curve period by leveraging on other people's experiences and attain your dreams much earlier than planned.

Other Forms of Leverage

vi) **Delegation** – Effective delegation is peradventure one of the most powerful high leverage activity in existence. You train your team transferring responsibilities to other trained and skilled people and they work for you in the long-haul while you devote energy on more highly-leveraged activities. Overall delegation translates to growth for both individuals and the organization.

vii) **Book Reading** – It's one of the best ways to rise to the top. You wouldn't need to reinvent the wheel since the great thinkers and wealthy business moguls have it all thought out for you. George Clason for example has done all the research on his book *"The Richest Man in Babylon,"* all you have to do is grab a copy or at the least download it and thoroughly go through it.

viii) **The Pareto Principle** – It's also known as the 80-20 rule (law of the vital few, and the principle of factor sparsity). The principle states that for a lot of events 20 per cent of the causes contribute to about 80 per cent of the effects. It was named after Vilfredo Pareto an Italian engineer, socialist, scientist, economist and philosopher. In 1906 he observed that 80 per cent of the land was owned by 20 per cent of the population; he arrived at the principle by observing that 20 per cent of the pea pods in his garden contained 80 per cent of the peas. It has been adopted as a common rule of business that 20 per cent of the products represented 80 per cent of the income. It's therefore widely accepted that a small percentage of the population will give a greater portion of the sales volume. It's fair therefore to assume that the 20 per cent represents the known customers who have already done business or will purchase your product or use your service within the next weeks, months or years.

Application of Optimal Leverage

The next form of leverage is;

i) **Acquisition of a team** – if speed is of essence then a competent team will enable you to achieve this.
ii) **Network** – the next form of leverage is getting numbers from the team. For example, if each member in a team of 10 knows 50 people, then put together it's a total of 500 people.
iii) **Infinite Network** – This comprises of the spiritual connection that links up humanity.
iv) **Tools and Skill-set** – Prosperous people utilize the tools of wealth – computers, e-mail, internet, smart phone–for quick calculations, communication and decisions. A good smart phone which can accommodate a great deal of the much required business apps is a plus and will go a long way in ensuring the smooth running and up to date communication for the overall success of the business.
v) **Systems** – In the present information age the internet is transforming how business is being conducted. Computer systems streamline and organize the whole process for success – connecting people, sharing information at a touch of a button churning out new millionaires every year. Good examples are online stores open providing 24/7 service 365 days a year reaching out to customers on the globe, a networking master setting up an online marketing campaign and travels around the world while his business continues to grow in his absence, CEO of a financial services group disseminating valuable concepts of a service at a product launch and reaching financial consultants around the globe in real-time using webinars.

Ultimate Thoughts:

The examples provided will make you comprehend how the successful and super rich people leverage on resources and that makes them get richer. It's all about delivering value, working smart by doing it intuitively, not working harder. It has everything to do with time and efficiency and overall establishing win-win situations.

CHAPTER 7

Plain-Old Dumb Luck

*"Once you make a decision, the universe conspires to make it happen – **Ralph Waldo Emerson***

A few moments of misfortune and chastisement could place wasted years of a vigorous fight on a downward spiral, and a few minutes of good luck could save you a stupendous amount of indefatigable hard work.

According to Prof. Richard Wiseman a psychologist at the University of Hertfordshire, CSICOP fellow and author of *The Luck Factor*, Barnett Helzberg Jr. was considered as a lucky man. By 1994 he had been able to establish an immeasurably prosperous chain of jewellery business outlets, which boasted annual turnovers to the tune of about US$300 million. On one fine morning while walking past New York's Plaza hotel, a woman called out aloud the name, "Mr. Buffett" to the man just right beside him and he overheard it. Helzberg battled within himself as to whether the man could have been Warren Buffett–one of the most prosperous investors in Northern America. Neither had he previously met him however, he had read about Buffett and the factors or financial scope he considers on acquisition of a company;

i) Durable competitive advantage over a considerable period of time.

ii) Honest to goodness and able management – because he won't manage it himself.
iii) Purchase price which is not excessive and looking out for exceptions.

Helzberg had then-turned sixty, and had considered selling off; when it occurred to him that indeed it could be the ideal company Buffett would take delight in. Helzberg seized the opportunity and crossed over to meet the stranger and made an introduction of himself. It then happened that indeed the man was Warren Buffett, and the fortuitous meeting turned immensely fruitful because about a year later down the line Buffett made an initial offer to acquire the chain of stores. And all this took place as a result of him walking down on a street in New York and a woman yelling out his name.

The story of Helzberg is a classic tale that demonstrates the influence of luck in business dealings. Nonetheless, good fortune rolls out in all facets of our lives and indeed plays an integral part.

Alfred Bandura a psychologist at Stanford has elucidated the effect of coincidental encounters and luck on individual's lives. Bandura took note of the occurrence and significance of this kind of encounters inscribing that, "some of the most important determinants of life paths, often arise through the most trivial of circumstances." Bandura's belief in these happenings is reinforced by his tell-tales and inference drawn from his personal life encounters. While at graduate school he once got stiff bored with a reading assignment and took off to a golf club in the locale with a comrade. As chance would have it, they found themselves in the company of two beautiful lady golfers and the two summed-up and turned four. Not long after the game, Bandura arranged another meet up with the lady and she went on to become his wife. His life completely transitioned following a meeting that just took place by chance at the golf club.

In summary, lucky occurrences have an immense impact on our lives. Luck is powerful and can transform the impossible into the possible, create a distinction between life or death, contentment and despondency, honour and destruction.

Force and Potency of Superstition

The Gallup Organization conducted a research on 1,000 individuals as to whether they were superstitious or not. From the findings 50 per cent were at least superstitious while 25 per cent confessed to being somewhat or very superstitious. Another study disclosed that 72 per cent of the commons admitted to possessing at least a single good luck charm.

Superstitious tendencies and beliefs have been handed down from generation to generation and one commonality in this thread is that people are cognizant of the fact that either good or bad luck can totally transform lives as well as reflect individuals appetite to look for ways to upscale their encounters with good luck.

Are Superstitions, Factual and a Creature of habit or is it just a Fallacy?

Many researchers have subjected superstitious beliefs to tests to validate them. One particular memorable one is high school students and members of the *New York Skeptics*, Mark Levin. The findings; one bottleneck – superstition doesn't work.

Superstition doesn't work because it's founded on age-old beliefs and an incoherent contemplation. It emanated from a period when individuals imagined that luck was a peculiar force that could be summoned into action by strange behavioural patterns and magical rituals.

Research on the Luck Factor

Ten years thereafter Wiseman chose to carry out a scientific research into the concept of luck

Wiseman set out to investigate and find out –why some individuals are constantly lucky while the others meet with few but misfortunate ones. In a nutshell, why are there individuals who experience lucky breaks and fortuitous encounters, while others encounter a never-ending tirade of tribulations.

The Findings

The revelation was that luck wasn't a magical capability and was also distanced from a chance occurrence. No one is borne lucky or unlucky. In contrast, both the lucky and unlucky individuals bear no insight into their actual causes of good and bad luck. However, their behavioural patterns and rationales are the driving force towards their fortunes.

Wiseman went on to reveal that lucky individuals propel their own streak of good luck through 4 basic guidelines;

i) They are knowledgeable at establishing and detection of chance opportunities.
ii) Select lucky choices by following their gut feelings.
iii) Establish and get attached to self-fulfilment prophecies by envisioning positive expectations.
iv) Assumption of a strong will and self-reliance that transitions bad luck into fortunate circumstances.

Opportunities by Chance

Lucky people consistently encountered chance opportunities when unlucky people did not.

Research revealed that the unlucky individuals were typically much more consumed in anxiety and tension than were lucky individuals. Studies have confirmed that the anxiety causes disruption in noticing the unexpected – unlucky individuals fall short of noticing chance opportunities because they are too concentrated in search of other things. For example they would attend to parties too focused on searching for their life partners and miss out on an opportunity to network and make friends. They skim through the newspapers looking for specific kind of job notices and miss out on other potential opportunities. Lucky people are more open-minded, easy and loosen up and that way they end up seeing more than what they are in search of.

Adoption of certain behaviours will intensify and heighten the amount of coincidental opportunities in individual's lives.

As Wiseman explains, "Imagine living in the centre of a large apple orchard. Each day you have to venture into the orchard and collect a large basket of apples. The first few times it won't matter where you decide to visit. But as time goes by it becomes more and more difficult to find apples in the places you have visited before. And the more you return to the same locations, the harder it becomes to find apples there. But if you decide to always go to parts of the orchards that you have never visited before, or even randomly decide where to go, your chances of finding apples will dramatically increase.

The same is applicable to luck. It's possible for people to drain all opportunities in their life by talking to the same people over and over again in the same manner. Continuing to use the same path to and from your place of work; carry on going to the same holiday destinations. Nonetheless, new and random occurrences present the prospects for new opportunities.

How to Cope When Bad Luck Unfolds

Psychologists allude to our capability to visualize what could have happened rather than what really took place as "counter-factual."

Lucky people seem to widely use counter-factual reasoning to cushion the emotional turmoil of a misfortune they encountered in their lives.

Wiseman went on to give an illustration to make it even more clearer, "I asked lucky and unlucky people to imagine that they were waiting to be served in a bank. Suddenly, an armed robber enters the bank, fires a shot, and a bullet hits them in the arm. Would this event be lucky or unlucky?"

Unlucky people went on to term it as tremendously unlucky and very unfortunate to be in the bank at the time of the incident. Contrary to this, the lucky people considered the scene and context as being extremely lucky and remarked unconstrained and impetuously on how the situation could have been far worse. One lucky contributor observed, "It's lucky because you could have been shot in the head – also, you could sell your story to the newspapers and make some money."

The distinction between lucky and unlucky was clear-cut and unmistakable. Lucky people are impulsively inclined to view unfortunate circumstances they go through could have been compounded and far much worse, and as a result they end up feeling better about life generally and as well as in their personal circumstances. This act in itself makes the lucky people maintain high future expectations and the probability of a continuous spree of luck following them everywhere they go.

Ultimate Thoughts:

Empirical analysis has blurted out that a great deal of the fortunate and unfortunate circumstances that we come up against are pretty much the making of our own behaviours and thinking. It significantly amounts to the likelihood of change to a set of what would have been considered a set of impossibilities – a powerful way of magnifying the amount of luck people are forced to contend with in their mundane world.

CHAPTER 8

What Dumb People are DOING that you're Not Doing: From Ordinary to Extra-Ordinary

"Lack of direction, not lack of time, is the problem. We all have twenty-four hour days." – **Zig Ziglar**

Think like the Rich, Improve your Cash Flow

Have you ever found yourself living pay check-to-pay check, there seems never sufficient funds to get around, incessantly short of money, always lagging behind in terms of what you required to do sometimes by US$20, US$50 or US$100, spending more than you earn, reaching out for more debt, sinking deeper and deeper in the hole.

The single greatest cause of unhealthy cash flow comes about as a result of poor management of pecuniary resources often arising out of ignorance, financial disregard and defiance or a combination of them all.

Cash Flow 101: Brushing through the Basics *(Never Taught in School!)*

The Fundamental Law of Money; to accumulate Wealth you MUST spend less than you earn.

To Resolve this Problem Permanently you could either Spend Less or Earn More or you Could Do Both.

> *"Annual income twenty pounds, annual expenditure nineteen nineteen and six, result happiness. Annual income twenty pounds, annual expenditure twenty pounds ought and six result misery." –*
> *Charles Dickens, David Copperfield*

The most important terms in investing and business are **Cash Flow**

Hitherto, according to Robert Kiyosaki, famous author of *"Rich Dad Poor Dad"* too many people are in financial distress and difficulty as a direct consequence of having too much money flowing out of their pockets and very little trickling into their pockets. To have a positive cash flow and secure your future, you will have to learn to retain more cash in your pocket than deluges out.

To improve the cash flow position you will need to have a shift of the mindset to focus more on needs instead of wants - as many of the things that are perceived as necessities really fall under the classification of luxuries.

- You don't need so many cable channels.
- Opt for public transport and drop the car.
- Do away with unnecessary contracts and the accompanying monthly outgoings.
- Don't buy things you can't afford.
- Increase your earnings – make extra income from your hobby, ask for a pay rise, find another job.

Typical Cash Flow of the Poor, Middle-Class and the Rich

1) *Cash Flow of the Poor*–All of their Income meets their living expenses and is still not sufficient - They are diligent and industrious, probably have two jobs but can hardly make ends meet, they leave pay check-to-pay check, they may have to incur debt to meet other obligations and have a hard-time getting through because they leave hand-to-mouth.

2) *Cash Flow of the Middle-Class*–Their income is channelled to meet their daily expenses, have few assets and have also acquired liabilities which they think are assets and have to keep feeding them – They fall in the category of the highest-earning in their field of expertise, have credit cards, cars and houses. They avoid investments but have retirement or 401(k) plans in place and spend their money making acquisitions of liabilities that don't put money in their pockets and that they also don't even need. Created a lifestyle that they have to either borrow more or find a higher paying job to be sustainable, they are perceived to be wealthy but are in financial difficulties and for the first-time are keen on personal financial education and are shifting their perceptions to those of the rich.

3) *Cash Flow of the Rich* –Have acquired earning assets and have income from property rentals, capital gains, dividends, passive income from businesses and residual income from royalties to fund their lifestyle – view the world from the perspective of an investor or business owner (not as an employee or self-employment) they have acquired financial knowledge and emotional intelligence in the information age, they feel financially secure and have attained financial freedom. The rich are on top of things and fully in control of where their money flows and they match the flow, before anybody else. The rich use debt to purchase apartment complexes where there is flow of people for high paying jobs – investment in real estate is not worthy if there is no movement of people for housing and so does money flow. Such information is not taught in school yet dumb people have access to it and are utilizing it to enrich themselves.

Now with this kind of information the answer lies with taking action. Until such a time that you decide to put the specialized knowledge into action is when your world transfigures.

"Power is described as the ability to act, while knowledge has been known to be potential power."– **Tony Robbins**

How to Draw Attention to your Business?

It's not too difficult to get attention. However, the kind of attention you are seeking will be the determinant of how you go about this all important exercise. People may laugh at you if you did something really silly, but bottom line is you got their attention and they will notice. Sir. Richard Branson the founder of the Virgin Group on launching Virgin brides was one of the rarest moment caught on tape having shaved off his beard, going bare faced with full face make-up and accoutred himself in a wedding dress. As Branson walked down the aisle for a cat-walk there was roaring applause, deafening wolf whistles and hundreds of cheers. *Dumb* isn't it? But it got known for a promotional campaign that caught the attention of the media and the information became common knowledge around the globe and indeed created to a great extent the much required buzz and awareness of the existence of the brand though owing to stiff competition the bridal and wedding wear founded in 1996 closed a year later.

Getting positive attention is much more difficult and entails doing something really outstanding for others for example, doing some CSR activity towards up scaling the services of a freedom house, volunteering to do some touch-up paint job on the youth hostel, street clean-ups, voluntary blood donations which also means really going out of your way to get the much needed visibility.

Entrepreneurs are discovering that standing out of a crowded marketplace requires some serious out of the box thinking and smart execution to capture the attention of your prospective clients. But above and beyond what matters the most and propels your marketing efforts and what ensures your survival in business, should be conversion of prospects into paying clients.

What Dumb People are DOING That You're Not Doing

I will share some really creative, thought-provoking, attention grabbing and prospect converting ideologies to revamp your marketing efforts and that can be tailor-made to fit the needs of your kind of business. These nuggets of wisdom will go a long way in ensuring your show of hits home with customers. They are applicable regardless of whether you want to leverage on social media and social media handles, creation of videos, promotional give-aways – bottle opener, metal key chains, corporate gifts; *unique power bank, branded coffeehouse mug and water bottle lanyard.* Stories of amazing customer service overtures fill the air - it's time to let your company be the story of the day.

1) *Fly your Freak Flag (Show a Character that is Hidden or Overt)* –By revealing your true self and showing everybody who you really are, some interesting qualities that single you out and are unique come into play. This could take the form of branding your fancy logo on your delivery vans and official cars, sharing photoshopped images of yourself in the company brochure, or write ups. Being vulnerable is one of the techniques that builds rapport in an instant yet it's the least

discussed and a very important attribute of a successful businessmen and salespeople. Actually when we become vulnerable, we share human qualities. Sharing vulnerability is usually the start of an open and genuine relation. Small things like these can make your website and business persona more pronounced, interesting and more easy-going and accessible which is good for business.

2) *MARKET LIKE CRAZY: How to Get As Many Clients*-You will need to understand a bit of the market psychology, know the mind of your target audience, really engage them and they will be eager to deal with you.
   a) Sponsor a community event.
   b) Socialize, get involved and participate in cultural, Church, school events, voluntary work and contributions.
   c) Attend meetings in your locality.
   d) Be visible and get listened to – comment on forums and blogs touching on your line of business.
   e) Print t-shirts, hats, pens, umbrellas and request them to be worn and used.
   f) Appear on TV interviews and get listened to on weekly complimentary sessions on radio.
   g) Pitch to your local county representative, congressman, Member of Parliament (MP) or Governor – blurt out what your business idea is all about.
   h) Come up with a tournament – contestants to take a picture with your company branded t-shirts and give positive vibes on your product or service.
   i) Establish networks for correspondences like newsletters, e-mail recipients, share updates on your Face book account and Twitter handle.

3) *Run Giveaways and Raffles*-You will need to be very clear and concise on what you want to get out of it...
   - Do you want to reward your present clients?
   - Is your motive to get more followers and clients?
   - Is it a memorable event you want to celebrate?
   - Are you priming an upcoming event?

Giveaways if done correctly are an inspiring way to appreciate your clients, promote your social media platform or blog and foster great client relationships and can increase the client base that you do transactions with.

4) *Show me the Money: Convert Visitors into Paying Customers*–The expectations are usually that a large percentage of visitors to your website would instinctively and unwittingly translate into more customers and increased sale, yet this isn't usually the case, what could be the reason?

   There is a reason behind why potential customers would land on a page and take off immediately: the main reason is the landing page and your inbound marketing strategy are not in synchrony and there's no focus; your offering isn't powerful coupled with long winded forms and about 90 per cent of web sites will use this in making their purchase decision. This means much thought has to be put into what you want the visitors to do within the first few seconds of landing on the page. You need to set the pace and lure your future customers.

5) *Accelerate your Success with a Trusted Partner*–Forging partner relationships with brands and entrepreneurs who are already established in the marketplace ensure that you drum for sales numbers not only effectively but also morally and economically.

6) *Power of Thinking Big: Unleash your Potential for Excellence*–Don't limit yourself to just social media, search engines or website traffic… Contact your local media and organize for a TV interview: they offer a unique opportunity to deliver messages to a wide audience spectrum swiftly and simultaneously. The Associated Press or your Local Press could even pick up the story depending on how innovative it is, but overall you get a major focus and get coverage on all nationwide newspapers.

7) *The Happy Customer: Improve Customer Satisfaction*–Forging meaningful bonds with clients creates a common ground, and as you foster relationships and add value they get drawn closer to you and sing your praises and deliver very powerful messages to your target clientele through introductions which ultimately lead to business.

   The clients and community provide value addition in the following ways:
   - *Networking.* New linkages widen exposure and heighten the referral base.
   - *Synergy.* The community presents shared experiences and resources that wouldn't otherwise be available.
   - *Partnership.* Like minded individuals are able to connect with an entrepreneurial mindset and with different strengths to compliment yours.

8) *Leverage on your Network*–An excellent method to get your name out there and get your fair share of hits home with customers is made possible through attending networking events. These kinds of linkages would leave word going round on online forums and publications and it would be discussed among the same people. This initiates more business and hits since if we were talked about in a positive way this is definitely something that would spur growth and gravititate the business to newer heights.
9) *Multi-tasking in Organizations: One-Stop-Shop*–A creative way to drive traffic to your website and subsequently clients and sales is by performing more than a single service. Demonstrate to your prospective clients or investors that you are a one-stop-shop and can deliver all beneficial services under *one* roof and in *one* invoice and *one* delivery note and *one* point of contact.
10) *Branding is Key to Business Success*–A customer's impression of a company and subsequent purchase decision whether knowingly or unknowingly is ultimately through scrutiny of the company's reputation, vibe and brand.

    Here are a few points to keep in mind while branding;
    - *Trust: The Most Powerful Currency in Business.* If the customers don't trust you, you are dead in the water; they simply won't buy from you. If they like your product or service but have trust and integrity issues with your company, they will look for someone else.
    - *Credibility: Your Most Important Asset.* What's the most salient selling feature of a company to the outside world? Stellar co-founders? An intellectual team? All these matter but credibility is the yardstick amongst which you and your company will be measured. It drives your ability to attract investors, raise capital and retain the committed and conscientious employees
    - *First Impressions are Key to Success.* Often times the first impressions about you are not your words but your look. Oh Yeah! Your Look. I know, it sounds quite unrealistic and biased, but in the first thirty-seconds people get perceptions about you on a subconscious level rooted on what they hear, see and sense, and every reason you must create a powerful visual first impact.

Your first impression with a customer ought to reflect your best intention and represent your brand whether it's an experience at the store, a marketing campaign or a trial with a product. Your brand must come out strongly in everything you do as well as in what the company depicts outwardly.

11) *It's All About the Follow Through: Converting Leads into Sales*– Sometimes the adage "Go Big or Go Home" is delusionary. Quiet light regular steps and personal touches on your network become the bedrock to building sustainable business. After meeting someone on a networking forum and you would like to meet them up, do the follow up, require an introduction from someone on your up line to further your business. Pick up the phone and make that call. Continue reaching out by phone, e-mails and personal notes. Keep the network and trust growing they are the first essential steps towards building a formidable business.

EPILOGUE

How do Dumb People Get to be so RICH?

It would be imprecise and fallacious to assume that Smart and Intelligent people cannot make loads of money. Being smart and gifted combined with a University degree could be an asset in most cases and can give you a head-start but not always. There are many people with high school diplomas combined with specialized training in their fields of expertise that have done very well for themselves and have made a fortune.

Have you peered into the eyes of the rich people and often-times found many of them quite dull? Have you ever listened to them and thought: "Other than money, what is it that they have that I'm not in possession of?"

The Illusion of a Brilliant Idea

The smart people conceive of one brilliant idea and are taken aback by a cognitive bias of overconfidence that makes them think–They are better than they actually are, they are better than others and imagine they know everything. The truth is that everyone makes mistakes. The Dumb people admit this fact and get ahead of others, but the Smart and Intelligent people do not, they are stuck in a comfort zone and hesitate when it comes to taking risks.

> *"I'm concerned that the fear of failing, in the eyes of the world, is the biggest impediment to amassing wealth."* – **Felix Dennis, Author of, "How to Get Rich."**

One "brilliant idea" won't get you rich yet. However, the Dumb know too well going to great lengths to execute the idea burying a ton of sweat, exerting oneself and doing one's best without sparing any effort could make you filthy rich. Anything that begins a discussion and builds a relation is considered social media and the idea existed even way before Mark Zuckerberg's invention. The difference is Zuckerberg went to great extents and endured pains, labour, sweat and combined it with new concepts and took a new angle that birthed Face book.

Luck Happens, But You can always Improve your Chances

When establishing, flourishing and being the proud possessor of a business, there will be many events, developments and end-results that can be influenced by luck. If you want to get riches, you will need to also have luck on your side

> *"Luck is what happens when preparation meets opportunity."* – **The ancient Philosopher Seneca.**

The more you are prepared, the more luck you attract and begin to make things drift towards you. Practice becomes second nature coupled with a good grasp of financial affairs, hands-on fiscal management and an unending quest for up scaling your knowledge and skill-set means that when the opportunities come your way, you are able to notice them much quicker and are financially apt to grab them in open arms and convert them into imperceptible and phenomenal wealth.

www.ingramcontent.com/pod-product-compliance
Lightning Source LLC
Chambersburg PA
CBHW021446210526
45463CB00002B/659